THE NORMAN CONQUEST
1065–1087

MICHAEL FORDHAM

The Schools History Project

Set up in 1972 to bring new life to history for school students, the Schools History Project has been based at Leeds Trinity University since 1978. SHP continues to play an innovatory role in history education based on its six principles:
- Making history meaningful for young people
- Engaging in historical enquiry
- Developing broad and deep knowledge
- Studying the historic environment
- Promoting diversity and inclusion
- Supporting rigorous and enjoyable learning

These principles are embedded in the resources which SHP produces in partnership with Hodder Education to support history at Key Stage 3, GCSE (SHP OCR B) and A level. The Schools History Project contributes to national debate about school history. It strives to challenge, support and inspire teachers through its published resources, conferences and website: www.schoolshistoryproject.co.uk

This resource is endorsed by OCR for use with specification OCR Level 1/2 GCSE (9–1) in History B (Schools History Project) (J411). In order to gain OCR endorsement, this resource has undergone an independent quality check. Any references to assessment and/or assessment preparation are the publisher's interpretation of the specification requirements and are not endorsed by OCR. OCR recommends that a range of teaching and learning resources are used in preparing learners for assessment. OCR has not paid for the production of this resource, nor does OCR receive any royalties from its sale. For more information about the endorsement process, please visit the OCR website, www.ocr.org.uk

The wording and sentence structure of some written sources has been adapted and simplified to make them accessible to all pupils while faithfully preserving the sense of the original.

The publishers thank OCR for permission to use specimen exam questions on pages 102–105 from OCR's GCSE (9–1) History B (Schools History Project) © OCR 2016. OCR has neither seen nor commented upon any model answers or exam guidance related to these questions.

Every effort has been made to trace all copyright holders, but if any have been inadvertently overlooked, the Publishers will be pleased to make the necessary arrangements at the first opportunity.

Although every effort has been made to ensure that website addresses are correct at time of going to press, Hodder Education cannot be held responsible for the content of any website mentioned in this book. It is sometimes possible to find a relocated web page by typing in the address of the home page for a website in the URL window of your browser.

Hachette UK's policy is to use papers that are natural, renewable and recyclable products and made from wood grown in well-managed forests and other controlled sources. The logging and manufacturing processes are expected to conform to the environmental regulations of the country of origin.

Orders: please contact Hachette UK Distribution, Hely Hutchinson Centre, Milton Road, Didcot, Oxfordshire, OX11 7HH. Telephone: +44 (0)1235 827827. Email education@hachette.co.uk
Lines are open from 9 a.m. to 5 p.m., Monday to Friday. You can also order through our website: www.hoddereducation.co.uk

ISBN: 978 1 4718 6086 7

© Jamie Byrom and Michael Riley 2016

First published in 2016 by
Hodder Education
An Hachette UK Company
Carmelite House
50 Victoria Embankment
London EC4Y 0DZ
www.hoddereducation.co.uk

The authorised representative in the EEA is Hachette Ireland, 8 Castlecourt Centre, Dublin 15, D15 XTP3, Ireland (email: info@hbgi.ie)

Impression number   10 9 8 7 6 5 4 3
Year   2024

All rights reserved. Apart from any use permitted under UK copyright law, no part of this publication may be reproduced or transmitted in any form or by any means, electronic or mechanical, including photocopying and recording, or held within any information storage and retrieval system, without permission in writing from the publisher or under licence from the Copyright Licensing Agency Limited. Further details of such licences (for reprographic reproduction) may be obtained from the Copyright Licensing Agency Limited, www.cla.co.uk

Cover photo © Getty Images/Danita Delimont

Typeset by White-Thomson Publishing Ltd

Printed and bound by CPI Group (UK) Ltd, Croydon CR0 4YY

A catalogue record for this title is available from the British Library.

MIX
Paper | Supporting responsible forestry
FSC™ C104740

CONTENTS

	Introduction	**2**
	Making the most of this book	
1	**Too good to be true?**	**8**
	What was Anglo-Saxon England really like in 1065?	
	Closer look 1 – Worth a thousand words	
2	**'Lucky Bastard'?**	**26**
	What made William a conqueror in 1066?	
	Closer look 2 – Battleground	
3	**'Brutal slaughter'**	**44**
	Is this how William gained full control of England, 1067–71?	
	Closer look 3 – Hereward the Wake – the last of the English	
4	**Military fortresses or status symbols?**	**62**
	What can research reveal about early Norman castles?	
	Closer look 4 – The Tower of London	
5	**'A truck-load of trouble'**	**80**
	What was the impact of the Norman Conquest on the English by 1087?	
	Closer look 5 – The Norman Yoke	
	Preparing for the examination	**98**
	Glossary	**106**
	Index	**108**
	Acknowledgements	**110**

Introduction

Making the most of this book

Where this book fits into your GCSE history course

The course

The GCSE history course you are following is made up of five different studies. These are shown in the table below. For each type of study you will follow **one** option. We have highlighted the option that this particular book helps you with.

OCR SHP GCSE B

(Choose one option from each section)

Paper 1 1 ¾ hours	**British thematic study** • The People's Health • Crime and Punishment • Migrants to Britain	20%
	British depth study •  The Norman Conquest • The Elizabethans • Britain in Peace and War	20%
Paper 2 1 hour	**History around us** • Any site that meets the given criteria.	20%
Paper 3 1 ¾ hours	**World period study** • Viking Expansion • The Mughal Empire • The Making of America	20%
	World depth study • The First Crusade • The Aztecs and the Spanish Conquest • Living under Nazi Rule	20%

The British depth study

The British depth study focuses on a short time-span when the nation was under severe pressure and faced the possibility or actual experience of invasion. The point of this study is to understand the complexity of society and the interplay of different forces within it. You will also learn

Introduction

how and why historians and others have interpreted the same events and developments in different ways.

As the table shows, you will be examined on your knowledge and understanding of the British depth study as part of Paper 1. You can find out more about that on pages 98 to 105 at the back of the book.

Here is exactly what the specification requires for this depth study.

The Norman Conquest, 1065–1087

Sections and issues	Learners should study the following content
England on the eve of the conquest Issue: The character of late Anglo-Saxon England	• The nature, structure and diversity of late Anglo-Saxon society • Religion in late Anglo-Saxon England • Anglo-Saxon culture: buildings, art and literature
Invasion and victory Issue: How and why William of Normandy became King of England in 1066	• Norman society, culture and warfare pre-1066 • The succession crisis of 1066 • The battles of Fulford, Stamford Bridge and Hastings
Resistance and response Issue: The establishment of Norman rule between 1067 and 1071	• First uprisings against Norman rule including resistance in the west and in Mercia • Northern resistance and William's 'Harrying of the North' • The rebellion of Hereward in the east and the end of English resistance
Castles Issue: The nature and purpose of Norman castles in England to 1087	• Pre-conquest fortifications and the first Norman castles in England • The distribution and design of Norman castles in England to 1087 • The purpose of Norman castles in England including their military and economic functions
Conquest and control Issue: The impact of the Norman Conquest on English society to 1087	• The Domesday Book, its creation and purpose • The social structure of Norman England including changes in land ownership and the elite • Changes and continuities: language, laws and Church

You need to understand the interplay between these forces in society:

- Political
- Religious
- Economic
- Social
- Cultural

You need to pay special attention to:

what lies behind the myth of 'the Norman Yoke' and should consider the extent to which the myth is a reflection of reality.

You should study a range of types of interpretation including:

- academic (historians)
- educational
- popular (e.g. television)
- fictional.

The next two pages show how this book works.

How this book works

The rest of this book (from pages 8 to 97) is carefully arranged to match wh
the specification requires. It does this through the following features:

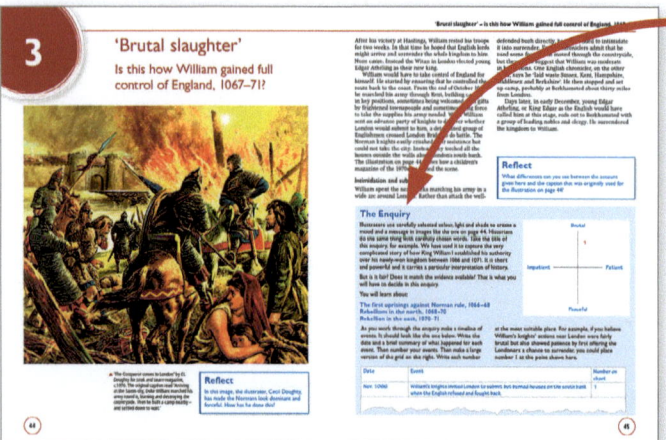

Enquiries

The book is largely taken up with five 'enquiries'. Each enquiry sets you a challenge in the form of an overarching question.

The first two pages of the enquiry set up the challenge a give you a clear sense of what you will need to do to work o your answer to the main question. You will find the instructions set out in 'The Enquiry' box, on a blue background, as in this example.

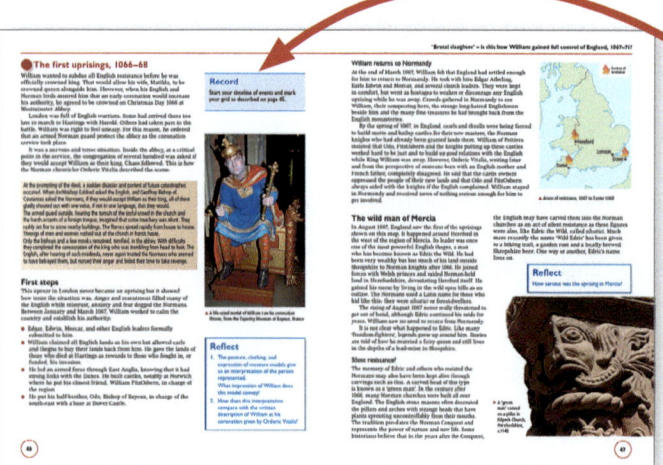

Record tasks

From that point, the enquiry is divided into three sections. These match the bullet points shown in the specification on page 3. You can tell when you are starting a new section as i will start with a large coloured heading like the one shown here. Throughout each section there are 'Record' tasks, whe you will be asked to record ideas and information that will help you make up your mind about the overarching enquiry question later on. You can see an example of these 'Record' instructions here. They will always be in blue text with blue lines above and below them.

Reflect tasks

At regular intervals we will set a 'Reflect' task to prompt yo to think carefully about what you are reading. They will loc like the example shown here.

These Reflect tasks help you to check that what you are reading is making sense and to see how it connects with wh you have already learned. You do not need to write down th ideas that you think of when you 'reflect', but the ideas you may help you when you reach the next Record instruction.

Introduction

Review tasks

Each enquiry ends by asking you to review what you have been learning and use it to answer the overarching question in some way. Sometimes you simply answer that one question. Sometimes you will need to do two or three tasks that each tackle some aspect of the main question. The important point is that you should be able to use the ideas and evidence you have been building up through the enquiry to support your answer.

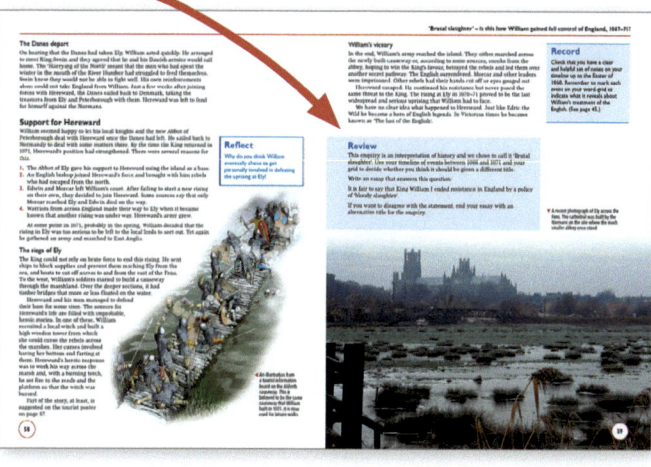

Closer looks

Between the enquiries you will find pages that provide a 'closer look' at some aspect of the theme or period you are studying. These will often give you a chance to find out more about the issue you have just been studying in the previous enquiry, although they may sometimes look ahead to the next enquiry.

We may not include any tasks within these 'closer looks' but, as you read them, keep thinking of what they add to your knowledge and understanding. We think they add some intriguing insights.

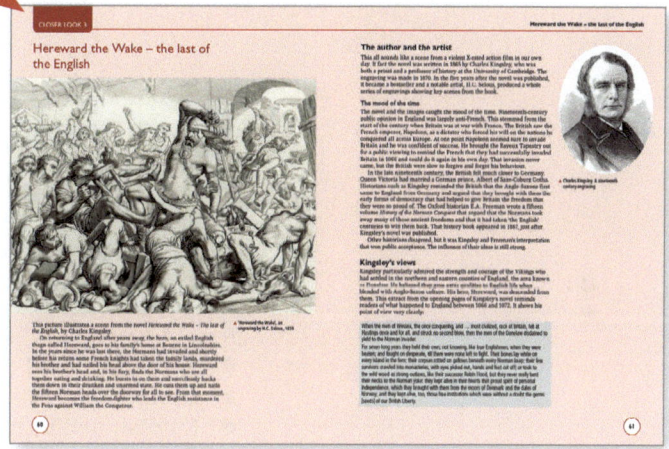

One very important final point

We have chosen enquiry questions that should help you get to the really important issues at the heart of each period you study, but you need to remember that the examiners will almost certainly ask you different questions when you take your GCSE. Don't simply rely on the notes you made to answer the enquiry question we gave you. We give you advice on how to tackle the examination and the different sorts of question you will face on pages 98 to 105.

King Edward of England instructs Earl Harold, one of his leading nobles, to visit Normandy, in France.

Earl Harold and his friends ride off to the south coast, taking with them their favourite hunting dogs. Harold is taking a fine hawk, held proudly above his horse's head.

▲ From the Bayeux Tapestry, c.1075

Embroidering the truth?

These are the opening scenes in the world-famous Bayeux Tapestry that was created in the eleventh century to tell the story of the Norman Conquest of England. The action moves from left to right.

There are some charming images here:

- the wise old king
- fine horses
- friends sharing a seaside meal
- English nobles baring their legs as they wade out to the boat with their favourite animals.

It is delightful ... but you would hardly believe the arguments that historians and others have had about the events shown in these scenes.

Some historians accept the story more or less as it stands. They point to written sources from the time that explain clearly how and why the King of England sent his most powerful earl across the English Channel to Normandy.

Other historians criticise their colleagues for taking the story at face value. They point out that there is not one single English source from the time that refers to any such visit. They insist that even though the tapestry was probably embroidered by English women, the scenes were all designed by Normans who wanted to give their own view of the Norman Conquest. The Normans may, quite literally, have been 'embroidering the truth' by adding to what really happened or by changing details to suit their own ideas.

Introduction

The group visit a church to pray before moving on to enjoy a meal in the house of a local lord. Someone at the door tells them it is time to leave.

They pick up two of their dogs and Harold's hawk, hitch up their tunics and paddle out to the boat. (You will learn what happened next later in this book!)

In this book you will be learning about some dramatic and intriguing events but you will also be studying different versions or interpretations of the past.

Why interpretations differ – some starters

Here are just three reasons why people may give us different versions of the same historical events:

1. **Problems with the evidence.** Sometimes, as in this case, the sources we use contradict each other or leave gaps. We have to mix careful, controlled thinking with creative, controlled imagination to deal with these problems, and that leaves plenty of room for honest disagreement.
2. **The context we work in.** Historians cannot avoid seeing the world with the values and the limitations of the age they live in. In the nineteenth century, for example, many English historians were affected by the anti-French mood that had continued since Britain's long wars against Napoleon. This often made them see the worst in the Normans.
3. **Drama and story-telling.** Historians are not the only people who write about the past. Sometimes novelists, playwrights and poets set their works in the past. So do artists and film directors. Sometimes they simply want to tell a dramatic story and the precise facts do not matter to them. At other times they may adjust what historians say about the past but still claim that they have done this to bring out a deeper truth about the historic situation or life in general.

But now, back to King Edward ...

> **Reflect**
>
> We have to use our imagination with historical sources to bring the past to life. For example, imagine the sounds and smells and feel of the scenes shown here.
>
> Compare your ideas with a partner.

1 Too good to be true?
What was Anglo-Saxon England really like in 1065?

▲ An illustration from a manuscript written c.1240

The saintly king

This picture is taken from a beautifully illustrated manuscript written in the thirteenth century. The book tells the life story of Edward the Confessor, who ruled England from 1042 to 1066, the years before the Norman Conquest. He is the only English king who has ever been declared a saint by the Roman Catholic Church.

This particular picture illustrated the story of how a poor, disabled Irish man called Michael once begged King Edward to carry him to the altar of Westminster Abbey. Michael was sure that he would be healed if Edward would only do this for him.

The saintly king lifted Michael onto his back and walked into the Abbey. As he did so, the blood from Michael's sores ran down the King's fine clothes. But as they approached the altar something remarkable happened: Michael felt life returning to his injured legs and the sores on his skin were healed. When the King put him down, Michael could stand for the first time in years. The poor man and his king rejoiced together by running and jumping around the abbey and singing hymns of praise to God.

The story is very unlikely to be true, of course. It reveals more about how later generations viewed Edward the Confessor than it does about actual events in his life. The King seems too good to be true.

A 'Golden Age'

In the same way that stories about King Edward have been exaggerated, so too has the reputation of the nation he ruled. Some historians believe that England was passing through some sort of 'golden age' just before the Norman Conquest of 1066 and that this was brutally and tragically ended by the invasion and rule of William the Conqueror. This view was particularly popular in the nineteenth century. Novelists, poets, artists and some (but not all) historians wrote about England on the eve of the Conquest as a land of free people, who could enjoy their fair share of its considerable wealth and who enjoyed an early form of democracy. As you will learn, this image of pre-Norman England is also too good to be true.

> **Reflect**
>
> Which parts of the story of King Edward and Michael surprise you most?

The Enquiry

In this enquiry you will learn about:

1. **Anglo-Saxon society** – the people and how they lived.
2. **Anglo-Saxon religion** – the Church and people's beliefs.
3. **Anglo-Saxon culture** – the art, literature and buildings of the time.

In each section you should make two lists. In one you should note anything that might have made life in late Anglo-Saxon England seem 'golden' to people who are determined to find the best in it. In the other you should explain why this interpretation of Anglo-Saxon England can be challenged. You will need to use evidence to support your explanations.

Record your ideas in a table like this:

Aspects of late Anglo-Saxon life that might seem 'golden'	Reasons why life was not really so 'golden'

Anglo-Saxon society in 1065

In 1065, the kingdom of England had only existed for just over a century. The character of different regions revealed how unsettled the land had been for centuries.

> **Record**
>
> Make the first entries in your table as described on page 9.
> Use the sub-heading 'Anglo-Saxon society'.

▼ Map of the Anglo-Saxon kingdom in 1065

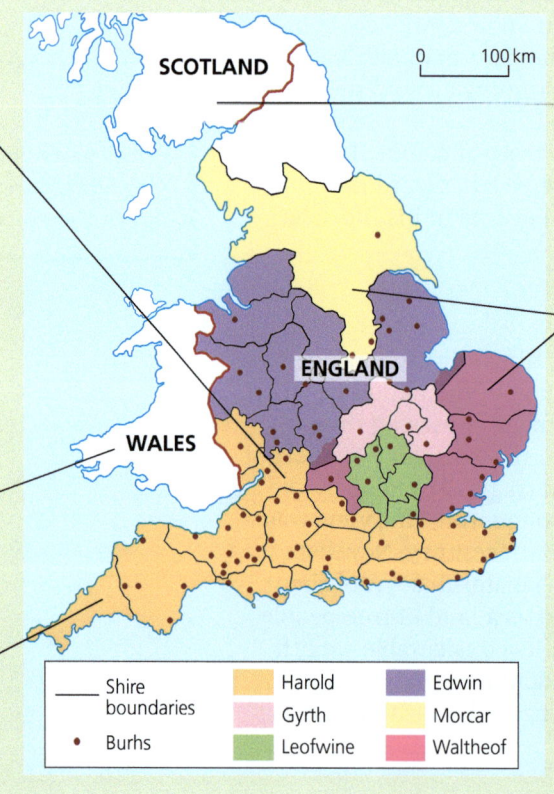

The people of the midlands and the south were mainly Anglo-Saxons. They settled there after arriving from northern Germany in the fifth century. Over time, they set up several different kingdoms such as Wessex in the south.

The people of Wales were descended from the British people who lived all over southern Britain until the Anglo-Saxons arrived. Wales had its own kings and kingdoms and was independent from England until the thirteenth century. The word 'Wales' is from an Anglo-Saxon word for a foreigner, outsider … or slave.

Cornwall had many of the ancient British people who had lived throughout the country until the Anglo-Saxons arrived in the fifth century AD.

Scotland was an independent country. The border region between Scotland and England was unsafe and unsettled. People made frequent raids into each other's land.

The people of the north and east of England were a mix of Anglo-Saxons and Vikings. The Vikings came from modern-day Norway, Denmark and Sweden and settled in these regions after about AD850.

The kingdom of England

In the tenth century, the rulers of Wessex led other Anglo-Saxon kings in wars to end Viking rule in the north and east. By AD954, the last Viking leader was defeated and England had become a single kingdom.

In France, kings struggled to control local lords who ran large regions as if they were private kingdoms. But, by AD1000, English kings had strong, central control. Their land was divided into shires. Most shires had several royal 'burhs'. These were fortified towns that kept the local community safe. This system was weaker in the north-east, but in most of England burhs developed, markets grew and trade prospered. Kings of England also supported trade by setting up royal mints that produced coins whose purity and value was trusted.

The system of shires, the success of trade and the steady supply of trusted coins made taxation in England far more efficient than it was in other European states.

From 1003, the Viking invaders returned. This time they defeated the English. Between 1014 and 1042 the kings of England were Danes, but they kept the system of shires, burhs and royal mints as it worked so well. England was one of the wealthiest and most efficient states in eleventh century Europe.

▼ Eleventh-century Anglo-Saxon coins

The people

Pages 11 and 12 describe the two million people who lived in England in 1065.

1. The king

The king had many powers and duties. He:

- owned more land than anyone else
- raised taxes to pay for the nation's defence and for the burhs, roads and bridges that encouraged trade
- issued new laws
- was responsible for justice in all courts of law
- was expected to be a fine warrior
- was responsible for the work of the Church (unlike kings on the continent).

When the last of England's Danish kings died in 1042, the man who took the throne was Edward the Confessor, an Anglo-Saxon. He never expected to become king and had spent 25 years of his early life in his mother's homeland, the Duchy of Normandy in France. He enjoyed hunting but he was no warrior. When he returned to England to become king in 1042, he concentrated his attention on Church affairs and left most royal duties to his closest advisers, some of whom were his French friends from Normandy.

2. Earls

The king's chief advisers were the earls. These earls and the leading bishops formed the Witan, a group of advisers that even helped decide who should take the throne when a king died. Earls could not keep private armies but they gathered and led the king's 'fyrd' (armed forces) in times of war. They also held shire courts twice a year.

By 1065, the six earls shown on the map on page 10, came from just three families. Their intense rivalry, plots and murders made England unstable and had almost caused a civil war earlier in Edward's reign. Harold Godwinson, Earl of Wessex, emerged as the richest and most powerful man in the kingdom. His sister Edith married King Edward. By 1065, Earl Harold effectively ruled England on Edward's behalf.

3. Thegns

Below the earls there were roughly five thousand thegns (pronounced 'thanes'). Their high status came from land ownership. A thegn needed to hold about 250 hectares of land. Some held even more. The richest one hundred might have direct contact with the king, but most just lived comfortably on their lands and carried out the king's work for him. They ran the local courts and collected taxes. They were expected to fight for the king if necessary. Although some created their own defensive burhs, they were not like the knights of France who had their own private castles.

▲ In this manuscript from c.1050, the King of England discusses royal affairs with his earls. Below them, thegns arrive on horseback at a royal burh

Reflect

1. Identify the King, earls and thegns in the picture.
2. From what you have read so far, what do you think were England's strengths and weaknesses in 1065?

Cutting and collecting timber. From a manuscript made c.1030

4. Ceorls

Ceorls (pronounced 'churls') made up the vast majority of England's population. Some had special skills as carpenters or blacksmiths but most worked on the land. They grew crops, kept animals and collected timber for building and firewood.

The better-off ceorls lived mainly in the eastern shires. They owned some land and a house of their own. However, most ceorls had to pay rent and do work for the thegn whose land they lived on. They had to serve in the king's 'fyrd' in times of war and they were also expected to repair roads and bridges. They were trusted to take part in local decision-making and trials in local courts.

Some people have seen ceorls as the backbone of a freedom-loving, early form of democracy. But, by 1065, ceorls were far less independent than they had once been. They were becoming more tightly bound to serve the thegn on whose land they lived and worked, and who protected them.

The remains of late Anglo-Saxon farming tools found by archaeologists at a site near Durham

5. Thralls or slaves

At the base of Anglo-Saxon society were the thralls or slaves. In most of Europe, slavery had died out by 1000 but it survived in England. Unlike ceorls, these people were the property of a master. They were not free to seek work elsewhere. Like animals, they could be branded or castrated. They formed about 10 per cent of the population of the country although the proportion was much higher in western shires. Some thralls were captured in war or were criminals. In times of famine, parents might sell a child into slavery. Anyone born into slavery remained a thrall.

Very little written evidence survives about the lives of thralls but a valuable source is *Aelfric's Colloquy*. This is a school book, written c.990, to teach Latin. It is filled with invented characters discussing their work. Here, a thrall describes his daily routine:

> I go out at daybreak, goading the oxen to the field, and I join them to the plough; no winter is so harsh that I would dare to lurk at home for fear of my master … Throughout the whole day I must plough a full acre or more … I must fill the stall of the oxen with hay, supply them with water and carry their dung outside. Oh! Oh! The work is hard. Yes, the work is hard because I am not free.

Reflect

1. Which of the artefacts (objects) above can you see in the image at the top of the page?
2. What do you think did most to affect the quality of life for ceorls and thralls?

What was Anglo-Saxon England really like in 1065?

Women

Historians have disagreed about the nature and quality of women's lives in late Anglo-Saxon England. The evidence is certainly confusing. Here are some statements about Anglo-Saxon women that have been used in books and articles on this subject. They are all true but do not give any single, clear message.

- Women had the legal right to own land and property. They lost this after 1066.
- Sermons from the time accuse gangs of men of buying female slaves, raping them and selling them on.
- Women had the legal right to leave a husband who committed adultery.
- Almost all written evidence about Anglo-Saxon women relates to higher status women known as 'ladies'. Skeletons of Anglo-Saxon women of lower status suggest that they must have done a lot of hard manual work such as churning butter, chopping wood and working in the fields at harvest time.
- In 'double-monasteries', where monks and nuns lived, worshipped and prayed alongside each other, the women were in charge.
- There were laws that set out fines for any sexual harassment of women.
- Five per cent of all the land in England was owned by women in 1066. Almost all these women were related to the earls.
- Cases of divorce were very rare indeed in Anglo-Saxon times.
- Women were in charge of their household stores and money. They did little work in the fields.
- 'Double-monasteries' had more or less ended by 1000.

The value of life

Under Anglo-Saxon law, every person had a cash value that depended on their social group. This was called a 'wergild'. If someone was killed, the person responsible would not be put to death if he or she could pay the correct 'wergild'. Values were expressed in shillings. (One shilling was roughly the value of a cow.) One eleventh-century document listed the values as:

King = 18,000 shillings
Prince = 9,000 shillings
Earl = 4,800 shillings
Thegn = 1,200 shillings
Ceorl = 160 shillings
Thrall = No value

▲ An Anglo-Saxon lady from an eleventh-century manuscript

The value of a woman was exactly the same as the value of a man who had the same status in society. If a woman was pregnant, her value was increased by 50 per cent.

Reflect

1. Which statements from the list above might support the idea that late Anglo-Saxon England was a golden age for women?
2. What is your own conclusion on the nature and quality of Anglo-Saxon women's lives?

Record

Continue to add notes to the table you started on page 9.

In particular, look for evidence about how free and how equal English people were in 1065.

Anglo-Saxon religion

In 1065, the English Church had a bad reputation but it had not always been like this. At the start of the eleventh century, its leadership and blend of traditions and styles had given it a unique quality.

The character of the English Church

In the lands that we now call Italy, Germany and France, the Church had spread from Rome. Over many centuries this Roman Catholic Church developed its own ways of working and its own styles of art, with an emphasis on saints and angels. The Roman Catholic Church was brought to England in AD597 and Anglo-Saxons, who had been pagans before then, became Christians over the years that followed. They adopted the traditions of the Roman Catholic Church.

In the north of England, however, a different Christian tradition had been spread by missionaries from Ireland. The Church there had its own forms of worship and its own artistic traditions. Its images avoided using straight lines and preferred to show elaborate patterns made up of interlaced bands, rather like the interwoven stems of plants.

The illustration on the right is from an English church manuscript that was made c.1012. It is written in Latin and it is the opening page of one of the Gospels, the part of the Bible that tells the story of Jesus. It blends the Roman Catholic and the Celtic traditions.

The English language

Another sign that the Church was different in England is that parts of the Bible were often written, not in Latin, but in English or rather 'Old English'. This is the form that was still spoken around the year 1000. Leaders of the Roman Catholic Church insisted that the Bible should only ever be written in Latin so that its accepted meaning should not get lost in translation. It is a sign of the independence of the English Church that monks continued to write Bible extracts in the normal language of the people.

> **Record**
>
> As you read pages 14–15, add entries to your table as described on page 9. Use the sub-heading 'Anglo-Saxon religion'.

▲ The opening page of John's Gospel from an early eleventh-century manuscript

> **Reflect**
>
> What signs can you see that this Bible illustration blends Roman Catholic and Celtic art?

What was Anglo-Saxon England really like in 1065?

The religion of the people

Very few English people could read. Gospels like the one on page 14 were for priests, monks, nuns or the wealthy and highly educated rulers of England. As so often in history, it is very hard to know what went on in the minds and hearts of the poorer people who made up the majority of the population.

Worship

We do know that in some parts of the country people gathered to worship around large stone crosses like the one shown here. In these places they may have had a simple shelter but they had no permanent church building. The English Church was more rural than it was on the continent. Some important Church centres were quite remote and they served as a 'hub' from which priests would visit outlying villages to lead the people in worship. It was only later, after the Normans arrived, that each village had its own stone church.

The Church all over England was proud of its own local traditions. The Pope in Rome complained that the English had too many saints who were often local people who were highly thought of after their deaths. In theory, new saints could only be made by the agreement of the Pope, but the English ignored this ruling.

Behaviour and belief

The English people may also have ignored or failed to live up to the Church's teachings in other ways. Records of sermons have some serious criticisms of standards of behaviour. People seem to have been fond of binge- drinking, over-eating and indulging in sex, especially on what were supposed to be holy days in the Church's calendar. One sermon said that the success of the Vikings' invasion in 1013 was God's punishment for the sins of the people of England.

Sermons also criticised people for belief in witchcraft and spells. In the days before the Anglo-Saxons became Christian, they had deep-seated beliefs in creatures such as elves and goblins that could do harm. In Anglo-Saxon Bible illustrations, the devil and demons are sometimes shown in forms that look very much like the elves from older pagan stories. They were often believed to be the cause of illness. Magical rings like this one are sometimes found. The symbols around the edge and on the inside have never been deciphered and historians believe that they are probably a spell or chant that was believed to ward off the evil spirits that might make someone unwell.

> **Reflect**
> 1. This stone cross was made in the north of England where Celtic Christianity was strong. How might you guess this from its decoration?
> 2. Some historians say that the sermon that criticised the behaviour of the English at the time of the Viking invasion proves that people were not deeply religious. Others disagree and say that a sermon of that type is sure to exaggerate. What would your own interpretation be?

◀ An Anglo-Saxon stone cross at Gosforth, Cumbria, c.900

▲ An Anglo-Saxon ring, c.900

Missed opportunities

At the end of the tenth century, England had some of the most impressive church leaders in Europe but their influence had not been allowed to flourish.

St Dunstan

Dunstan was a monk from Somerset who became Archbishop of Canterbury in AD960. He spent hours in prayer but also devoted himself to art. He was highly skilled as a musician, an engraver and an illustrator. The image shown here was almost certainly drawn by him. It shows the figure of Christ. Many historians believe that the monk kneeling humbly at Christ's feet is a self-portrait of Dunstan. He was generous and unselfish. Once, when a powerful Anglo-Saxon lady left Dunstan a fortune, he spent it all on improving the monasteries of England.

Dunstan set the English church high standards.

- He worked to end corruption and greed among church leaders.
- He worked to improve the education and commitment of the priests, monks and nuns.
- He insisted that priests should not marry.
- He organised the rebuilding of many churches, abbeys and monasteries, often helped by donations from local thegns or earls who wanted the monks and nuns to pray for their souls.

Soon after he died in 988, English Church leaders declared Dunstan to be a saint. They would probably have continued the church reforms of Dunstan but, at the start of the eleventh century, England was again suffering from raids by Vikings. In 1011 these raids destroyed much of Canterbury.

It was the war and disruption caused by this wave of Viking raids that ended the great achievements of the late Anglo-Saxon church. The Danish kings who ruled England between 1014 and 1042 were Christians and they did support the church, but it never recovered the strength that it had in 1000.

King Edward

The English church missed another opportunity to reform itself during the reign of King Edward the

▲ The figure of Christ, from a tenth century manuscript

Confessor. Having spent his early life in Normandy, Edward knew the high standards that the Church was setting itself on the continent. He brought Norman priests to England when he became king. One of these, Robert of Jumièges, became Archbishop of Canterbury in 1051 and he set about improving the church, despite resistance from English priests. The image on page 11 is from a manuscript that Robert created to train monks in high-quality illustration.

In 1051–52 there was a power struggle in England. Godwin, who was Earl of Wessex at the time, objected to the rising power of Edward's foreign-born friends and forced the King to replace Robert with a new Archbishop of Canterbury. His name was Stigand.

Stigand

This picture of Archbishop Stigand was woven into the famous Bayeux Tapestry. It gives his name in Latin.

Stigand became a priest as a young man. He impressed people more for his skills of efficient administration than for any spiritual gifts. He did little to try to improve the quality of the church or the priests. Instead he served the King and Earl Harold as an adviser.

By 1065, Stigand was both Bishop of Winchester and Archbishop of Canterbury. Holding two church positions at once and being paid for both was called the sin of 'pluralism' but Stigand refused to give up the post as bishop. He was also accused of 'simony', selling off church posts to the highest bidder. This was the sort of corruption that St Dunstan had tried to end.

Stigand kept his influence because he had the support of Harold Godwinson, the Earl of Wessex. With Harold's support, Stigand gained land in ten shires and became very rich indeed, making some generous gifts to churches and monasteries.

In Rome, the Pope, who was head of the whole Roman Catholic Church, was deeply upset. He insisted that Stigand had to give up his post at Winchester and come to Rome for an official blessing. Stigand ignored him and stayed in England.

> ### Reflect
> What does the story of Stigand tell you about the condition of the Church in Anglo-Saxon England by 1065?

More problems with priests

The leader of the Church in the north of England was Wulfstan, Archbishop of York. He was a more spiritual man than Stigand and spoke out against slavery, for example. But, like Stigand, he broke the rules by being both Archbishop of York and Bishop of Worcester. He, too, was close to Harold Godwinson.

Below the archbishops and bishops were the thousands of priests who worked across the nation. Compared with most of Europe at the time, many English priests were poorly educated. The Pope also criticised the English Church for allowing its priests to marry, something that had been discouraged on the continent for hundreds of years. In the eyes of the Pope, this was another sign of the backwardness and low standards in the English Church in 1065.

▲ Archbishop Stigand from the Bayeux Tapestry c.1075

> ### Record
> Complete the entries in your table as described on page 14.

Anglo-Saxon culture

Some historians have emphasised the quality of art, literature and buildings as evidence of an Anglo-Saxon 'golden age'.

> ### Record
> Start the final section in your table as described on page 9. Use the sub-heading 'Anglo-Saxon culture'.

▲ The Alfred Jewel – an impressive piece of Anglo-Saxon art

In 1693, a ploughman working in a field in Somerset noticed something golden shining in the upturned earth at his feet. When it was cleaned, the gold shined even brighter and the intricate shapes and patterns of the metalwork were found to hold an enamel image of a man carrying what seem to be two long-stemmed plants. Around the edge some words are engraved in Old English: 'ALFRED MEC HEHT GEWYRCAN'. This means 'Alfred had me worked (made)'.

Within a few years, the jewel had been handed over to the Ashmolean Museum in Oxford where it has been kept ever since. Most experts now believe that the jewel was once attached to a long and slender wooden pointing-stick that would have been used to identify words and images in old manuscripts. It probably belonged to a monastery. Some believe that it was one of several such pointers that were sent around the country in AD890 by Alfred the Great, the King of Wessex who started the English fightback against the Vikings at the end of the ninth century. In the opinion of many, it is the single most impressive work of art from Anglo-Saxon times, a sign of remarkable skill.

> ### Reflect
> Do you think an object made c.890 can be used as evidence of a 'Golden Age' in Anglo-Saxon England on the eve of the Norman Conquest?

What was Anglo-Saxon England really like in 1065?

Art

Some of the finest art produced in Anglo-Saxon England involved engraving. You have already seen how they engraved the stone cross on page 15 and the borders of the Alfred Jewel on page 18. Here are two more examples.

The Fuller brooch

This is the Fuller brooch, named after the person who owned it for many years. Like the Alfred Jewel, it was made at the end of the ninth century. It is a brooch made of silver. It represents the five senses:

- Sight is shown in the centre where a man stares out at us with his eyes open wide.
- Taste (above and to the left) has his hand in his mouth.
- Smell (above, on the right) has his hands behind his back as he stands surrounded by tall plants.
- Touch (below, to the right) is rubbing his hands together.
- Hearing (below and on the left) lifts a hand to his ear.

Anglo-Saxon objects like this are very rare. Precious metalwork and books decorated with gold and jewels were stolen from England, first by the Vikings and then by Normans. Even later, Anglo-Saxon religious art was often destroyed when Henry VIII dissolved (ended) the monasteries.

We have evidence that Anglo-Saxon England was still famous for its metalwork and engraving skills in the 1050s when an English chronicler from the abbey at Evesham praised the Abbot there as a great craftsman in metalwork. One Norman chronicler mentioned how foreign merchants travelled to England to buy works made by English craftsmen. He described English men as 'outstandingly skilful in all the arts'. He added that English women were highly skilled at weaving with gold thread and at embroidery. We can see this in the Bayeux Tapestry which was embroidered by English women on the orders of their new Norman masters.

A case

Anglo-Saxons also did delicate engravings in other materials. This small case is about 23 centimetres long and has a sliding lid. It is made from walrus ivory. The top and sides have been carefully engraved by hand with figures such as dragons, lions, birds of prey as well as human hunters. The base has scenes from archery and farming. It may have been made to hold quill pens or perhaps a musical instrument.

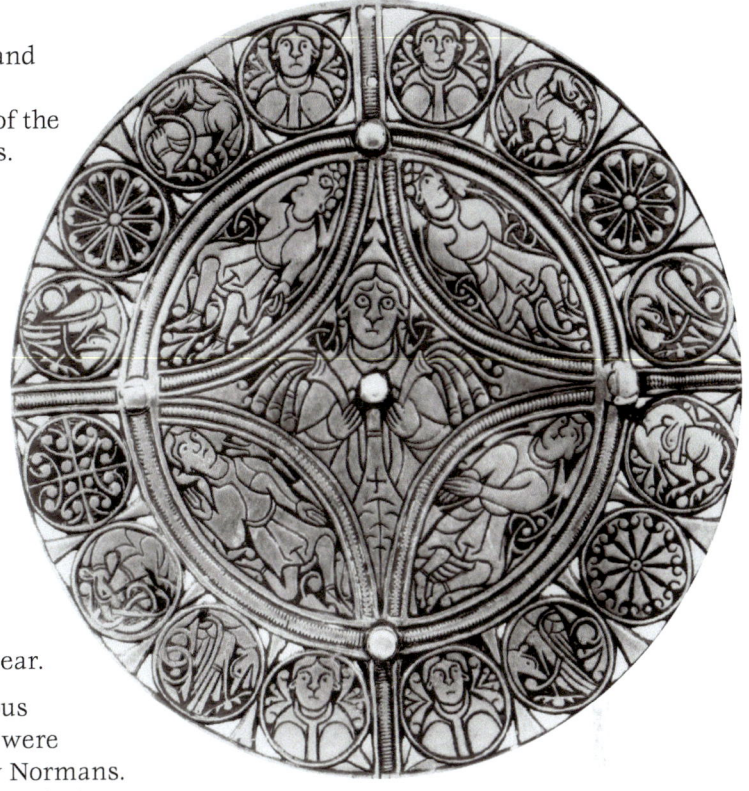

▲ The Fuller brooch, c.890

Reflect

Some art experts believe that the figure in the Alfred Jewel on page 18 represents the sense of sight. Would you agree?

Reflect

What does this case, with all its engravings, suggest about life in Anglo-Saxon England?

◀ An Anglo-Saxon case from the late eleventh century

Literature

You have already seen images from books made in Anglo-Saxon times on pages 11, 13, 14 and 16. These are all from Church manuscripts but the Anglo-Saxons' literature was rich and varied.

'Science'

The image of men collecting wood on page 12 is not from a religious document. It is from a calendar that is found in a curious semi-scientific manuscript written around the year 1000. It contains a map of the world, information about astronomy and a description of far off places called 'Marvels of the East'. The image opposite shows two of the many strange creatures that were believed to live in the east. One is half man and half lion. The other is a giant, eating a human being.

The 'Marvels of the East' was originally created in ancient Greece and was then kept alive by the Romans. This version is written in Anglo-Saxon Old English.

Fiction

The most famous Anglo-Saxon work of fiction is 'Beowulf', a poem that is over three thousand lines long. It was first written down sometime between AD700 and 1000. It is set in Scandinavia, the home of the Vikings, and it tells the violent story of how a warrior named Beowulf hunts down and slays a monster and then the monster's mother. Even if it was not originally written in late Anglo-Saxon times, the poem was certainly still popular then. Like most literature from the time, it would have been spoken out loud for an audience rather than read by an individual. The story is still read today in its original form or in modern translation. It has even been made into a television series.

History

At the end of the ninth century, probably on the orders of King Alfred the Great of Wessex, monks wrote a history of Britain that started with the arrival of Julius Caesar. Copies were made and sent to monasteries around England. The monks then updated the history in their books independently until the twelfth century.

Historians call the full collection of these histories the *Anglo-Saxon Chronicle*. It can be very one-sided and

▲ A page from an eleventh-century manuscript showing 'Marvels of the East'

has many gaps, but it is a really valuable source and it shows how the Anglo-Saxons had a growing sense of their identity as a nation.

Miscellany

Many surviving works of Anglo-Saxon literature mix sermons, poems, biographies of saints, medical treatments or advice on grammar. The largest known collection of Anglo-Saxon writings is the *Exeter Book*. This contains a mixture of works compiled in the late tenth century. It is owned by Exeter Cathedral but it contains far more than religious writings. Its most famous entries are Anglo-Saxon riddles, some of which are simply too rude to include in a school textbook today!

Reflect

What does the literature described on this page suggest about the interests of Anglo-Saxon people?

What was Anglo-Saxon England really like in 1065?

Buildings

The Anglo-Saxons built almost entirely in wood, clay and straw. In fact, the Old English word for a builder was 'timbrend'.

As the buildings were made of wood, they have all rotted away. Archaeologists have investigated Anglo-Saxon sites and can work out the shape of the houses and other buildings from the slightly different soil in post-holes. These are where upright timbers once stood. As they rotted away, the soil that built up inside was of a different colour from the surrounding area. They show the shape and give some idea of the size of the building by the thickness of the uprights. Most Anglo-Saxons lived in rectangular, single-storey houses with thatched roofs, but thegns lived in larger houses with two floors.

Even though they were often made of wood, some Anglo-Saxon buildings were remarkably fine. We know this from written descriptions, often recalling what a building looked like before it was burned down. With timber walls and thatched roofs, fire was a constant threat. One eleventh-century writer praised a nunnery at Wilton in Wiltshire. Although it was fairly small, he compared it with the temple of Solomon that is described in the Bible. It had fine wooden carving, beautifully painted plasterwork, a winding staircase, polished precious stones and golden ornaments. He also delighted in the quality of the garments worn by the nuns, another reminder of the English skills of weaving and embroidery.

Burhs

There were only three castles in England by 1065 and these had all been built very recently by the friends of King Edward who had brought the design from Normandy. Far more common were the royal burhs that were built all over England (see page 10). These were surrounded by walls to keep the local community safe from attack. A few of these were made from stone, usually in towns originally built by the Romans. One of these was London or Londenburh, as it was called by Anglo-Saxons. Winchester was the capital of England in late Anglo-Saxon times but London was the largest burh and was growing in importance.

In most cases, however, the burh was defended by large earthworks of ditches and ramparts, with a strong wooden barrier. The photograph below shows the remains of a section of the Anglo-Saxon earthworks at Wallingford in Oxfordshire.

> **Reflect**
>
> How useful is the photograph of the thousand-year-old defensive earthworks at Wallingford for someone studying Anglo-Saxon burhs?

▼ Remains of the Anglo-Saxon burh defences at Wallingford in Oxfordshire. Photograph taken in 2006

Churches

◀ St Peter's Church, Barton-upon-Humber

The only stone building that most Anglo-Saxons would ever enter would have been a church. Even though some still gathered for worship around a stone cross (see page 15), many villages had built first a timber and then a stone shelter in which to worship. Over the centuries most of these have been pulled down and new, larger, stone churches have taken their place.

In some cases, such as this one at Barton-upon-Humber, the original Anglo-Saxon building was kept with later additions being built as extensions. In this photograph, the tower and the small section to its left are Anglo-Saxon. Everything to the right, as well as the top section of the tower, are from later periods.

The tower often served as a place of protection for the people and housed a church bell that called people to worship or gave warnings.

The ground floor of the tower was where the people stood for worship. The section on the left was a 'baptistry', set aside for baptisms. A similar-sized area on the right of the tower was where the priest stood at the altar to lead worship. It was demolished long ago to make room for the extensions on the eastern side of the church.

◀ An artist's reconstruction of how the church may have looked c.1050. Drawn c.2000

To give some idea of how the church may have looked in the eleventh century, just before the Norman Conquest, an artist has produced this drawing.

Historians think this church, like many at the time, was built by a thegn as a private chapel. This was increasingly common by the eleventh century. The Anglo-Saxon preference for building in wood can still be seen in this stone building: the various arches and pillars that can be seen on the wall of the tower are made in stone but are purely decorative. They provide structural support for the building. They are like the shapes that would have been visible in a timber-framed tower.

On the continent of Europe it was far more common to build with stone. The great St Peter's church in Rome was the finest in western Europe. One architect has suggested that its floor space may have been as much as 600 times bigger than the average Anglo-Saxon village church. Closer to Britain, the Normans in France had built many large and strong stone churches in their own distinctive style. Church-building clearly was not the Anglo-Saxons' greatest artistic achievement, although there was at least one notable exception, as you are about to learn.

Reflect

Are you surprised the church building at Barton-on-Humber was so small in the eleventh century?

What was Anglo-Saxon England really like in 1065?

▲ Westminster Abbey and Westminster Palace as they may have looked c.1065. A reconstruction by artist Terry Ball, c.1990. The artist has shown a 'cut-away' view of parts of the abbey to show its interior

Westminster Abbey

We end this enquiry where we began: with King Edward the Confessor and Westminster Abbey. Edward was fond of spending time in London and built a palace at Westminster, just a few miles down the River Thames from the main burh.

The palace stood where the present-day Houses of Parliament can be seen. An abbey already existed just a few hundred metres away. With the advice and help of his Norman friend, Robert of Jumièges, King Edward paid for a new abbey to be built in the style that was so popular in Normandy. It was longer and taller than any other Anglo-Saxon church. It was made from carefully cut stone and had rounded arches in the Norman style. Little remains of that abbey today as it was more or less completely rebuilt in the thirteenth century, but in the last years of his reign King Edward had spent much of his time making it as splendid as he could. It was his own effort to show that Anglo-Saxon England was one of the great nations of Europe.

1066

The official opening of the great new abbey was held on 28 December 1065. Unfortunately King Edward was too ill to attend. The new year arrived with the English king on his deathbed. It was to be a year unlike any other in English history.

Reflect

What made Westminster Abbey such an impressive building?

Record

Complete the entries in your table as described on page 18.

Review

In 2008, a book was published with the title *The Battle of Hastings: The Fall of Anglo-Saxon England*. The book's author, Harriet Harvey Wood, argues that the late Anglo-Saxon period in English history was 'wonderful and astonishing'. How far do you agree with her? Use the notes you have made in this enquiry to help you to explain your answer.

CLOSER LOOK 1

Worth a thousand words

On the opposite page, you can see two artistic reconstructions of the past. You saw two of these in the last enquiry and you will find many more throughout this book. These reconstructions are not based purely on imagination. They are important interpretations of history and the artists who create them must work with the evidence available.

We find artistic reconstructions in museum displays, guidebooks, information boards at historic sites, history books and archaeological reports. The artists who create these images have to keep four big questions in mind.

What is the point? (Purpose)
It could be one or more of these:
- to show the appearance of a particular site at a particular time
- to show an imaginary but typical site based on real ones
- to show how the site worked and what people did there
- to show how the site fitted into the landscape or the rest of society
- to give a quick, clear impression
- to draw the viewers into spending time taking in the details of the scene.

How do you know? (Research)
It must never be based on guesswork, so artists should:
- do their own research
- meet experts, such as archaeologists and historians
- visit the site (preferably with the experts)
- ask awkward questions of the experts; for example, about lighting in rooms or colours of walls and clothing
- keep the notes from the research to help others later
- find ways to show which parts of the picture experts are not so sure about.

Who is it for? (Audience)
It could be one or more of these:
- family groups visiting a site together
- children learning about a site as part of a school project
- foreign tourists from many different countries
- academic experts needing very accurate detail with no distractions.

How can you help the viewer? (Technique)
Use different methods to achieve different effects. For example:
- scenes at eye level make the viewer feel more involved
- aerial views help to show wider context; for example, the landscape or variety of activity
- cut-away walls and roofs show life inside buildings or architectural details
- fade-out in grey any parts of an image that there is less evidence for
- use colour to add warmth and to make the scene lifelike
- create a mood or atmosphere, e.g. by the weather, or keep it neutral if that is more appropriate
- surprise the viewer with true details they would not expect; for example, women doing work normally associated with men
- include people to give a sense of scale
- show people in detail to add life, show clothing or how work was done
- show people with little detail if you do not want them to distract the viewer
- add photographs of archaeologists at work or of artefacts found at the site to help the viewer understand the sources that the illustration has used.

Reflect
1. How many of these techniques can you see being used in the artists' reconstructions on pages 21 to 25?
2. Which techniques do you find particularly helpful?

Worth a thousand words

◀ An Anglo-Saxon home and everyday activities, Canterbury Archaeological Trust, c.2010

▼ Portchester Anglo-Saxon burh, c.1000. This burh was one that started as a Roman fort so it uses more stone than most

25

2 'Lucky Bastard'?
What made William a conqueror in 1066?

Statue of William the Conqueror in Falaise, France. By Louis Rochet, 1851

What made William a conqueror in 1066?

This monument stands in Falaise in northern France. The main figure on horseback is William, Duke of Normandy, who was born in the town in 1028. After his death in 1087, he became better known as 'William the Conqueror'.

William's statue was erected in 1851 and some years later smaller statues were made to stand beneath his feet. These show William's six predecessors as dukes of Normandy. They are:

- Rollo the Walker (so-called because he was a giant of man and no horse could carry him)
- William Longsword
- Richard the Fearless
- Richard the Good
- Richard III (who did not rule long enough to win a good name)
- William's father, Robert the Magnificent.

The people of Normandy obviously liked a good nick-name! Statues and names given to leaders after their death are two more examples of interpretations of history. They try to capture and share something about the person in question. In William's case it is just as well that the statue uses the name he was given after his death, rather than the one he was most commonly known by in his lifetime. He was born to a young woman called Herleva who was probably the daughter of a local undertaker, although no one is sure. Duke Robert, William's father, never married Herleva and from an early age his only son was known as 'William the Bastard'. Despite this unpromising beginning, as he was Robert's only son, the 'Bastard' was allowed to inherit the Duchy of Normandy. He went on to overshadow all his ancestors. They were dukes but he became a king – King William I of England.

Reflect

The person who made this statue has tried hard to give the impression that William was a mighty and fearless leader. How has he done this?

The Enquiry

In this enquiry you will learn how William achieved his remarkable success and decide how he was able to become King of England. Maybe you will agree with the historian John Gillingham. In 1996, after carefully studying William's career and how he managed to defeat Harold at the battle of Hastings, Gillingham decided that William was, in fact, very fortunate to take the English throne. He recommended that William should really be remembered as 'William the Lucky Bastard'.

This enquiry will focus on William's invasion and conquest of England in 1066. You will see that there is plenty of room for disagreement between historians over several points in the story and you will need to make up your own mind about each of these. The story will unfold in three sections:

1. **Norman society, culture and warfare by 1066**
2. **The succession crisis of 1066**
3. **The battles of 1066 at Fulford, Stamford Bridge, and Hastings.**

In each section you must make a list of key points that helped William gain victory over Harold. These points should be gathered under the following headings:

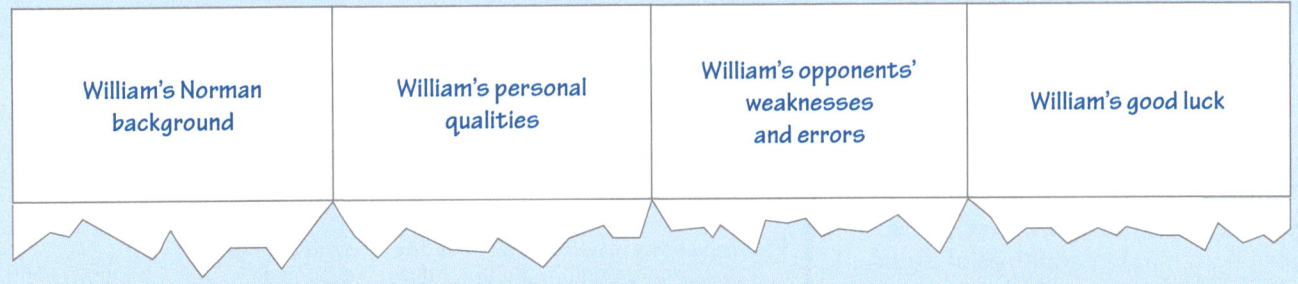

William's Norman background	William's personal qualities	William's opponents' weaknesses and errors	William's good luck

Normandy in 1065

As you can see from the map, Normandy lies in northern France. However, strictly speaking, there was no such country as France in the eleventh century. A 'King of the Franks' ruled the lands within the red boundaries shown on the map, but these were not called France until the thirteenth century. In England, the struggle to drive out the Vikings had led to the development of a single kingdom where the King had strong central power over all his lands. The King of the Franks had far less central control. The only lands that he could claim to rule directly were those shown in purple on the map.

The feudal system

The other areas outlined within the red boundaries on the map were ruled by dukes or counts on behalf of the King. These duchies or counties were known as 'fiefs'. The duke or count who ruled these were 'vassals', men who had sworn loyalty to the King of the Franks. The King then granted the fief (lands) to them and they, in return, promised, amongst other things, to use their own armies to fight on behalf of the King.

Historians call this arrangement of land-holding in return for service the feudal system. It sounds similar to what happened in England but the important difference is that although English armies were gathered by the earls and thegns they were the King's armies. In France, dukes or counts had their own armies that they promised to use for the King when necessary. This gave French dukes and counts considerable independence. They ruled their lands rather like private kingdoms.

> **Record**
> Start making your notes as explained on page 27. You should find points to include under the first two headings..

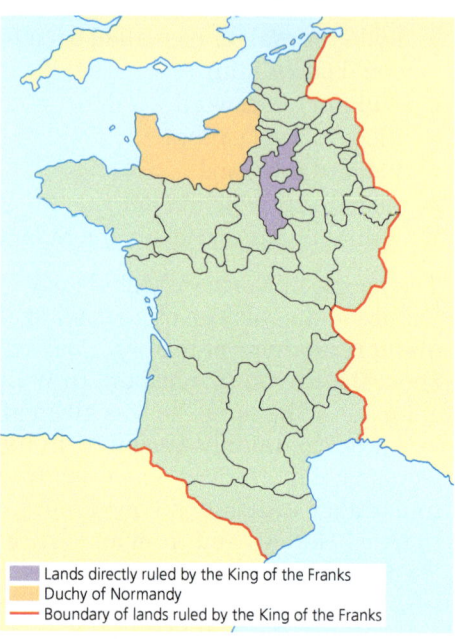

■ Lands directly ruled by the King of the Franks
■ Duchy of Normandy
— Boundary of lands ruled by the King of the Franks

▲ France in 1035

The strength of Normandy

Normandy was one of the strongest fiefs in France. It had started as a Viking colony in the early tenth century when Viking raiders sailed down rivers and struck deep into northern France. Its name means 'Land of the Northmen'.

The Vikings' first leader in this new French settlement was Rollo the Walker, whose statue stands below William's in the photograph on page 26. In AD911, having taken the land, Rollo became a vassal of the King of the Franks. Over the next century he and his descendants doubled their territory by conquest and by marriage alliances. They used brutal force to crush any rebellions but they also adopted the language, laws and forms of government of the French people they now ruled. They chose trusted men as local lords who governed each part of the duchy. By the time William the Bastard was born in 1028, Normandy was, in many ways, more stable than many other areas of France.

▲ Viking boats attacking northern France. A nineteenth-century painting

> **Reflect**
> In this painting, the artist has tried to show the speed and power of a Viking raid. How has he done this?

▲ Knights fighting. A stone carving made c.1120

Knights

Viking raids were based on the speed of their ships and the fierce use of battleaxes and swords. In France, a different but even more effective form of warfare was developing.

As dukes and counts across France tried to build up the strength of their private armies, they started to provide loyal supporters with armour and weapons and to keep them as full-time soldiers. With their chain mail, swords and shields, these professional soldiers would have been a frightening force, but their greatest strength was that they had mastered the art of fighting on horseback. In France they were called 'chevaliers'. We know them as knights.

New forms of fighting

The invention and spread of the stirrup helped this form of warfare to develop. It allowed knights not only to charge their enemies on horseback, but to remain on the horse leaning out and swinging their swords while still fixed firmly in the saddle. The Anglo-Saxons never took to this way of fighting. In the 1050s, one of Edward the Confessor's Norman friends who had been granted some land in the west of England, tried to get the English to fight on horseback against the Welsh. It was a hopeless failure. To fight this way needed years of training. William did not invent it, he just grew up among men who had mastered the technique and who could put it to good use when he later led the invasion of England in 1066.

This image shows two knights fighting each other with lances. Historians argue about whether Norman knights at Hastings used these weapons in this way or whether this approach developed later. In the Bayeux Tapestry, most knights seem to be throwing spears.

'Thugs'

Whatever their methods, the eleventh-century knights of France were a long way from being the 'knights in shining armour' of fairy tales. One historian has said that 'some of them were little better than brutal thugs'. This does not simply describe their approach to fighting; it covers their general way of life. They, too, were part of the feudal system. Just as dukes and counts received fiefs as vassals of the King, so these knights swore to serve their lord (the duke or count) and received land in return. They then used their own military power to take as much tax and rent as they wanted from the people who lived on the land under their control.

Reflect

What made knights so effective in battle?

Castles

Knights had to defend the precious land that gave them their wealth. They did this through the use of castles. Some were made from stone but most were made of earthworks and timber like so many royal burhs in Anglo-Saxon England. But the similarity ends there. The castles of French knights were not made for the defence of the wider community. They were a knight's home and fortress in one. They were made to keep themselves and their fellow warriors safe and to provide a safe 'hub' from which they could ride out and dominate the area.

There were two main types of castle.

▲ A model reconstruction of an eleventh-century French knight's castle at Le Plessis-Grimoult

1. The older and simpler form was a 'ringwork' castle. It consisted of an enclosure called a 'bailey' surrounded by a ditch and an earthwork bank topped by a strong wooden fence. The entrance, which would always be the weakest point, was fortified by a solid gatehouse.
2. The new and particularly effective form was a 'motte and bailey' castle. This was similar to a ringwork, but within the bailey there was a man-made mound known as the motte. On top of this motte a wooden structure called a 'keep' served rather like a castle within the castle.

Both types of castle could be built with great speed. Knights who took new land or who dared to rebel against the authority of their lord, could set the local people to work to construct a basic fortress in a matter of days, although larger ones might take a few months to complete. Over time, the wooden defences would be replaced by stone walls and keeps, but only if the knight had succeeded in establishing his rule in the area.

▲ A model reconstruction of an eleventh-century French knight's castle at Grimbosq

Normandy – stability and strength

Although the power of knights was growing in Normandy, they were carefully controlled by the different dukes who followed Rollo. This made Normandy much more stable than other parts of France at the time when William was growing up there. But knights were always hungry for land and power and would soon challenge any weakness shown by their lords.

Reflect

The two models above are both interpretations of eleventh-century castles.

1. How are they different from each other?
2. Why do you think they are different from each other?

Christianity and the Church

The first Vikings in Normandy were pagans who believed in many different gods. When he became a vassal of the King of the Franks, Rollo converted to Christianity. In the years that followed, his descendants put pagan ideas behind them and, with Viking energy, they built up the strength and quality of the Roman Catholic Church in their lands. While England was drifting from the high standards it had set around 1000, Normandy was moving to the forefront of Roman Catholic reforms, building many fine new monasteries. Popes praised Norman monks and nuns for their devotion, their teaching and their art and music. Above all, Normandy became famous for the beauty of its churches.

This photograph shows the interior of an abbey in Caen, the Normans' capital city. Its height and the elegance of its fine rounded arches are typical of the Norman style of architecture that was being copied across much of continental Europe at that time. It was called 'Romanesque' as the rounded arches were similar to those used in the Roman Empire many centuries before. Even fairly humble town churches in Normandy were made from stone and featured this same style, while many English churches were still made from wood.

Normandy was becoming both settled and wealthy, with firm government, efficient taxation and strong trading links around northern Europe. And yet, soon after William was born in 1028, it faced a crisis.

▲ The Abbaye aux Dames in Caen, Normandy

William's early experiences

In 1035, when William was just eight years old, his father died. William became the new Duke of Normandy but he was far too young to rule. Almost immediately, Norman knights turned against each other and grabbed land and power for themselves. They built castles and challenged authority, unsettling the duchy. Senior lords ruling Normandy on behalf of William were killed in battle or simply murdered. The new guardians who took their places may well have been the murderers. William learned to be careful whom he trusted.

As he grew older, William took a more active part in trying to restore order. By 1047, when another large-scale revolt was taking place, he took command. He skilfully negotiated with the King of the Franks who helped him to crush the rebels. William proved to be a good tactician and a fearless soldier. In the style of the first Viking dukes of Normandy, he could be merciless to his defeated enemies in the aftermath.

William grew in experience as he increased his control and his territory. He defeated enemies in battle and, like Rollo years before, he made a very useful marriage alliance. He took Matilda of Flanders as his wife in 1050. Flanders was a powerful county that bordered Normandy.

William and Matilda knew that their marriage was against church rules as they were distant cousins. They were both deeply religious and, as a way of thanking the Pope for giving them special permission to marry, they each built an abbey in Caen. You can see the interior of Matilda's abbey above. Building started there just as work on Westminster Abbey in England was coming to an end. It is at Westminster Abbey that we continue the story in the next section.

Reflect

What links can you find between the story of 'William's early experiences' and the information about Norman society on pages 28 to 31?

Record

Complete the notes you have been making on this section (pages 28 to 31).

Remember to use the headings given on page 27.

The succession crisis

> **Record**
>
> Continue making notes under the headings given on page 27.

Edward the Confessor dies. From the Bayeux Tapestry, c.1075

In January 1066, Edward the Confessor lay on his deathbed. The upper part of this scene from the Bayeux Tapestry shows him with his closest friends. At the foot of the bed his wife Edith wipes away a tear. Immediately below that scene, the tapestry shows him again. The Latin says he is *defunctus*: he is dead.

As Edward had no children, it was uncertain who would rule England after him. The events of 1066 were shaped by what the King may have said in his last moments.

Dying words

We simply cannot be sure what Edward actually said as he lay dying. The sources from the time are unclear. A biography of Edward was written for Queen Edith soon afterwards. It names the four people who were by his bed as his servant, Robert, his wife, Queen Edith, Archbishop Stigand and Earl Harold. It describes how he praised Edith, then reached out to Harold and said 'I commend this woman and all the kingdom to your protection'.

It is not clear from this whether Edward meant Harold to rule England as King or just guard the country and Edith until a new King was crowned. Historians are not even sure whether Edward ever spoke these words at all. The biography was written for Edith who was the sister of Harold Godwinson. Harold's claim to the English throne depended entirely on these deathbed words from Edward.

With so little clear and trustworthy evidence, and with this being such a dramatic and significant moment, different writers have summarised Edward's dying words in different ways:

> **Reflect**
>
> 1. How do these three interpretations differ?
> 2. Why do you think they summarise the King's death so differently?

From www.historyinanhour.com 'History for busy people', 2016

Edward offered his hand to his brother-in-law Harold, and placed the kingdom of England into his protection. After these important announcements, Edward fell back into a coma and died during the night of 5 January 1066.

From *Edward the Confessor* by professional historian Frank Barlow, 1984

Even if Edward did recover consciousness just before the end, speak with a loud voice and make some sensible remarks, it is extremely doubtful that his mind was in a fit state to make a bequest. Moreover, we must admit that pressure could have been put on the dying man to say what was required, or words uttered indistinctly could have been interpreted by the archbishop in the sense he wanted.

From a novel, *The Last English King*, by fiction writer Julian Rathbone, 1997

Queen Edith knelt and put her ear close to the lips of the King. His throat rumbled like dry wattle in the wind, a bubble of spittle formed between his lips and burst. The King farted. The king died.

Queen Edith stood up tall, looked down into the hall, spoke clear and loud like a trumpet, her voice filling all the spaces.

'My lord the King is dead'. She took a breath. 'These were his last words. "I do prophesy the Witan will choose Harold Godwinson to rule England in my place. He has my dying voice."'

What made William a conqueror in 1066?

The claimants

Harold Godwinson was not the only person with a claim to be Edward's successor. He had three potential rivals. This chart shows where they all came from and why each one might have been crowned King of England. The crowns show the kings of England and the order in which they came.

In eleventh-century England, the throne did not automatically go to the nearest living relative of the King. Ideally, the person who would take over needed to meet the following criteria:

- be in the 'bloodline' of the previous king (that is being directly related)
- be chosen by the previous king
- be chosen by the Witan (leading nobles).

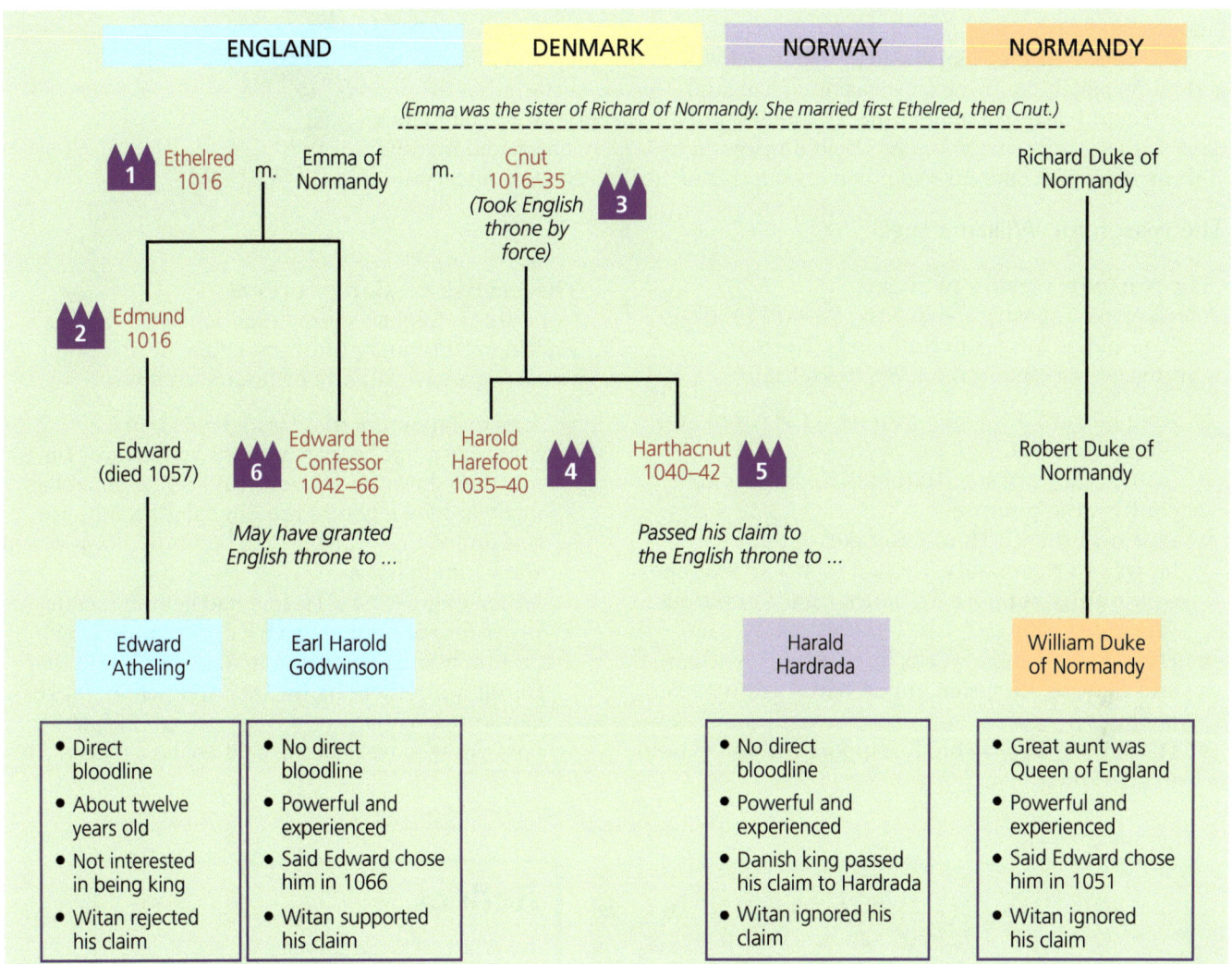

The new king – Harold II

Earl Harold Godwinson wasted no time. He persuaded the Witan that Edward had granted him the throne and the nobles then agreed that he should be king. This is probably what is happening on the far right of the picture on page 32. Two nobles meet Harold and hold out a crown and a battleaxe. The two men may well be Edwin and Morcar, the brothers who were Earl of Mercia and Northumbria respectively. Harold won their support by agreeing to marry their sister, a deal which would strengthen their family's power. Without their support, it is unlikely that Harold could have become king.

On 6 January 1066, just hours after King Edward was buried in Westminster Abbey, Harold was formally crowned as the new King of England. He had his crown. He would soon need his battleaxe.

> **Reflect**
>
> Based on the criteria listed at the top of the page, how strong were the claims of each of the four claimants shown on the diagram?

Responses to Harold's coronation

On learning that Harold had been crowned King of England, each of the three other claimants reacted differently:

Edgar accepted the situation. He knew he was too young to rule and that he had no power base in England, having been born in Hungary where his father went when the Danes took the English throne. If he had pushed his claim by his royal blood, maybe the story of 1066 would have been very different.

Harald Hardrada, King of Norway, had his hands full at the start of 1066 as he had been fighting a war against the Danes. He took no immediate action to follow up his claim to the English throne, but he became involved later in the year.

William, Duke of Normandy, responded with silent fury and immediate action: he began planning an invasion of England. He was certain that the crown should have passed to him. To understand his reaction, we need to look back to the events that you read about on pages 6 to 7. They happened in either 1064 or 1065. The date, like so much else in this critical episode, is uncertain.

The reason for William's anger

The Norman version of events

The Bayeux Tapestry shows King Edward sending Earl Harold of Wessex to Normandy. Norman chroniclers writing in the 1070s insist that:

- King Edward originally promised the throne to William in 1051.
- In 1064, Edward sent Harold to Normandy to confirm the promise.
- Edward ordered Harold to take an oath while he was in Normandy. He had to swear that he would fully support William's right to take the English throne.
- Harold spent some weeks hunting with William and fighting alongside him in battle against his enemies.
- Harold willingly swore to support William's claim to the crown.

The English version of events

Not a single English source mentions any visit by Harold to Normandy until the 1120s. At that point two writers gave slightly different accounts:

- A historian wrote that Harold did go to Normandy, but he was not sent by Edward. He was there because he went out fishing on a boat that was blown across the English Channel. He was forced to swear his oath before William would allow him to leave.
- A monk agreed that Harold had been forced to swear his oath but he gave a different reason for him being in Normandy. The monk said that Harold went there by his own free will because he wanted William to release two of Harold's relatives who were being held hostage there.

Harold swears an oath in front of William. To add to the power of the oath, he touches boxes of relics, probably the bones of saints. From the Bayeux Tapestry, c.1075

Reflect

1. Which of these accounts do you think is most likely to be true and why?
2. If Harold did swear an oath, was that a sign of weakness?

What made William a conqueror in 1066?

Any of these accounts could be true. It is quite possible that King Edward sensed that Harold wanted the throne for himself. By sending him in person to confirm that William should be the next King of England, Edward could also insist that Harold should swear the oath of loyalty while he was in Normandy. If this really is what happened, then William could thank Edward for his foresight. The Duke won lots of support for his invasion of England by claiming that Harold had broken a promise made before God. If, on the other hand, Harold came to Normandy purely by accident or for some personal reason, he played right into William's hands.

When historians are faced with contradictory sources like this, they have to use their wider knowledge of the situation to decide which ones 'ring true'. They may reach very different interpretations though, as in these two examples:

> **From *The Normans and the Norman Conquest* by R Allen Brown, 1985**
>
> That King Edward ... sent Harold to confirm the earlier promise of the succession to Duke William is entirely consistent with what is known of his Norman sympathies and wishes ... As for Harold, if the mission was unwelcome to him it would have been nonetheless difficult to refuse, and he may have been motivated also by the thought that if he did not undertake it his brother would.

> **From *The Norman Conquest* by Marc Morris, 2016**
>
> By 1064, Harold and his brothers reigned supreme, whereas the authority of Edward the Confessor had been eroded to virtually nothing. It stretches credibility ... to believe that the King, aged and powerless as he was, could have commanded the earl to do anything that would damage his own interests, let alone to help revive a scheme for the succession to which he had always been opposed.

> **Reflect**
>
> How and why do these two interpretations differ?

William's preparations for invasion

Whatever had happened when Harold was in Normandy, William was determined to take the English crown. With characteristic energy and an eye for detail, he set about planning an invasion of England.

He quickly sent men to Rome to win the support of the Pope. They described Edward's promise to William, Harold's oath and how he had broken his word. They told the Pope how Archbishop Stigand crowned Harold, knowing that he saw Stigand as the sign of all that was bad about the English Church.

The Pope gave his full and open support. He sent them back to Normandy with a papal banner to carry into battle as a sign that God was on their side. William used the Pope's support to win over the many who, very reasonably, doubted whether the invasion could succeed. He also offered great rewards to those who backed him. His Norman vassals were obliged to fight for him but he gained extra support from other powerful men across northern France in this way.

Spring was spent building extra ships and moving armour, weapons, food and wine to the coast. In the summer, foot soldiers, archers, knights and horses made their way to a great camp at Dives-sur-Mer. By early August, William's invasion force was ready.

▼ William's army prepares to invade England. From the Bayeux Tapestry, *c*.1075

> **Reflect**
>
> What supplies are being transported in this picture?

> **Record**
>
> Complete the notes you have been making on this section (pages 32 to 35).
>
> Remember to use the headings given on page 27.

The three battles

> **Record**
>
> Start the final section in your notes under the heading 'The three battles'. Keep using the headings given on page 27.

In England, King Harold's spies told him about William's invasion fleet. Just as he was starting to organise his defence of England, there came a worrying sign. In April 1066, the *Anglo-Saxon Chronicle* recorded the appearance in the night skies of a 'long-haired star' that stayed for over a week. We now know that this was a comet that reappears every 76 years, but at the time the English took it as terrible omen of a disaster that was soon to come.

Just as the comet was disappearing, news of violent raids along the south coast of England reached Harold. These attacks did not come from Normandy. They were led by one of Harold's own brothers, Tostig. He had lost his place as Earl of Northumbria in 1065 and was probably trying to force Harold to reinstate him. His attacks moved up the east coast but were never a serious threat and he was driven away in May 1066. Despite the comet, the country seemed safe once again.

▲ From the Bayeux Tapestry, c.1075

The Battle of Fulford

The *Anglo-Saxon Chronicle* says that Harold raised more in taxes than any other king. He used the money to pay for the fyrd (army) and a fleet to defend the south coast of England. By June 1066, thousands of Englishmen were based along the south coast, watching for an attack from Normandy.

They were still waiting in early September. Nothing had happened. Provisions were running out and the men were desperately needed on the land to bring in the harvest. On 8 September, believing that William's own men would have to bring in the crops in France, Harold disbanded the fyrd. Almost immediately, another army landed far away in the north-east of England. Tostig had returned, this time with the support of Harald Hardrada, King of Norway. After fleeing the country, Tostig had travelled to Norway and had persuaded Hardrada to invade England and take the throne.

When Harold heard the news he hastily gathered an army in the south and marched north. Meanwhile, on 20 September, the northern earls, Edwin and Morcar, led a force into battle against the invaders at Fulford, just south of York. The *Anglo-Saxon Chronicle* records the outcome:

> They fought army against army and made great slaughter. A great number of the English were slain or drowned or driven in flight and the Norwegians had possession of the place of carnage.

▲ The battles of Fulford and Stamford Bridge

> **Reflect**
>
> By 20 September 1066, do you think most English people would still have thought the comet was a sign that England was doomed?

Edwin and Morcar escaped but nothing could stop Tostig and Hardrada taking the city of York. The invaders rested there with the clear intention of moving south to claim the rest of the kingdom.

What made William a conqueror in 1066?

The Battle of Stamford Bridge

On 25 September 1066, Harald Hardrada and Tostig moved their army out of York to a nearby river-crossing called Stamford Bridge. They were probably waiting there to receive the surrender of other Anglo-Saxons from the area before heading south. They had no idea that King Harold had managed to gather his army again and had marched the two hundred miles from London to York in barely a week. He had increased the size of his force as he went along and the fleet had also carried more men up the east coast.

Harold had expected to have to attack Hardrada and his brother Tostig in York. On finding that they had left the town, he marched his combined force straight through from one side to the other and launched a surprise attack on his unsuspecting enemies at Stamford Bridge. The Norwegians were not even wearing their chain mail as it was a warm day.

Despite King Harold's advantages, the two armies fought for many hours before the Norwegians surrendered. It was the last ever hand-to-hand battle on British soil. Thousands died on each side. Hardrada and Tostig were among them. After the battle, Hardrada's son, Olaf, was allowed to sail back to Norway having promised never to return. His father had brought three hundred ships but no more than twenty-four were needed for the voyage home.

▼ The Battle of Stamford Bridge, painted by Peter Nicolai Arbo, 1870

Painting the past

In 1870, a Norwegian artist painted this interpretation of the Battle of Stamford Bridge. His name was Peter Nicolai Arbo and he specialised in military paintings and scenes from Norse mythology. This combined both.

He based the image on the 'Saga of Harald Hardrada' a tale written c.1230 by an Icelandic poet called Snorri. Nineteenth-century historians used to think that Snorri was a reliable source about historical events but he is no longer trusted as his sagas rarely match other sources or the findings of archaeology. Snorri tells us, for example, that the English fought on horseback at Stamford Bridge but they only did this after the Norman Conquest. The artist has followed Snorri's account here, though, and King Harold is shown in white swinging his sword as Hardrada, in the centre, dies a hero's death when an arrow pierces his windpipe.

> ## Reflect
> 1. Was King Harold lucky to defeat Hardrada and Tostig?
> 2. Why do you think the artist has placed Hardrada, not King Harold, at the centre of this painting?

The Battle of Hastings

King Harold must have believed that he had saved his crown after his victory at Stamford Bridge. He was still at York just days later, probably on 1 October, when news reached him that William's army had landed on the south coast, not far from Hastings. Clearly the Normans had not disbanded their army to bring in the harvest after all.

William's wait in France

William's army had been on the French coast for about six weeks before finally sailing to England. The long delay had been difficult to handle. The force of about 7,000 thousand men included between 2,000 and 3,000 knights with their horses. They came from many different regions in northern France so there might have been disagreements. They all needed food and water and William gave strict orders that they were not to raid nearby villages or farms. Instead he ensured they had all they needed. One of the French chroniclers, William of Poitiers, praised the discipline of William's army:

> Weak or unarmed, any man could move about the district at his will, singing on his horse, without trembling at the sight of soldiers.

▲ The Normans set sail for England. The carved figure of a boy blowing a horn at the rear of this ship shows that it is the one that was specially made for William by his wife Matilda. The person at the front may be William. In the ship behind his back, you can see some of the knights' horses. From the Bayeux Tapestry, c.1075

Poitiers explained that the reason for the long delay was bad weather and the wind that blew constantly from the north. There was no chance of sailing across the English Channel until it changed direction. He describes how William did once attempt to set off in bad weather on 12 September. This resulted in the ships being blown a hundred miles east along the coast. Many were wrecked at sea. William set up a new camp where the wind had taken them. The army spent two weeks there. William arranged an open-air service where the whole army prayed around the bones of a saint that had been brought out of a tomb. The army finally crossed to England, probably on 27 September.

▲ Pevensey and Hastings

Reflect

Some historians have suggested that William deliberately delayed his invasion so that King Harold would eventually have to disband his army. Do you agree with them?

William's strategy in England

On 28 September, William landed at Pevensey. He learned that King Harold had gone north to fight Hardrada. He chose not to move inland, but quickly built defences at Pevensey and Hastings. He now encouraged his men to raid the surrounding area. This helped provide for their needs but William was also probably deliberately trying to provoke King Harold's anger by pillaging the King's own lands. It may have worked: on 13 October, William's spies informed him that Harold's army was hurrying towards Hastings.

What made William a conqueror in 1066?

King Harold's haste

Harold rode south from York to London in just four or five days. His foot soldiers could not match this pace so he sent out orders for new troops to gather in London and in Sussex, near Hastings. His brother, Gyrth, and his mother both urged him to stay in London until he had a full army. He angrily rejected their advice and headed for Hastings, probably on 11 October.

Some historians say that Harold was hurrying because he was enraged by William's brutal plundering of Sussex. Others say Harold was simply trying to repeat the surprise attack that had worked at Stamford Bridge.

Despite his haste, Harold still failed to surprise the Normans. William's lookouts saw him coming and at dawn on 14 October, the Duke marched out towards Harold's army. This was a much smaller force than it might have been. Many experienced soldiers had died at Stamford Bridge; some were still in the north; others from the south were trying to join him but were still many miles away. Even those who had ridden south with him must have been weakened by tiredness or injury.

Harold had to find a battleground that might give him an advantage. He chose to take his stand on a short ridge with a forest behind it. This would make any orderly retreat impossible but it favoured a strong defensive line. The chosen site was about seven miles from Hastings. When they saw the site, many English deserted.

The battle begins

Early in the morning on 14 October 1066, the armies prepared to do battle. William prayed and, according to one chronicle, he wore around his neck some of the holy relics on which Harold had sworn to help him become king. He arranged his archers, infantry and his knights on horseback at the foot of the hill.

At the top of the hill, King Harold had a force of about the same size, 7,000 men. If he had waited longer, he might have had twice as many. None was on horseback. Some were 'housecarls', more or less professional warriors who served the king, but most were thegns and freemen from the shires. They stood in a line about 400 to 600 yards long and twelve men deep, with their shields forming a wall in front of them.

At nine o'clock, trumpets sounded and war cries filled the air. The battle was under way. The Norman archers fired a hail of arrows and, under this cover, the Norman infantry made their way up the rough slope as the English hurled javelins and stones at them. Once the Normans reached the top, they swung swords and axes to try to break the English line. It held firm. The Norman cavalry then got involved. They could not charge up the slope so they simply rode to the front line, sat on their horses and battered English heads with swords and clubs. Even after hours of this, the English line still refused to break.

> ## Reflect
> 1. How far does Ivan Lapper's painting below match the account of the battle on the left?
> 2. What may explain any differences?

▼ The Battle of Hastings painted by Ivan Lapper, c.2000

William's 'retreats'

After hours of stalemate, a group of Norman knights turned away from the battle line and rode back down the hill. Some English soldiers chased after them. At the same time, a rumour went around that William had been killed and the Normans too began to drop back.

This was a crisis for William, but he quickly pulled back his helmet and rode along the Norman lines. He showed his face, called out that he was still alive and reminded his men that there was no way back to France: they had to win or die. He led a counter-attack against the English who had charged down the hill, killing them all. One French chronicle says this 'retreat' was a trick by some knights that nearly backfired, but others say they really were on the run.

Several Norman chroniclers say that William later ordered his knights to fake two more retreats so that the English would once again break their lines and follow. They did and were cut down like the first group.

For years many historians insisted that no army of that time feigned retreats. They said the French chronicles were just trying to cover up panic in William's army. Then other historians found examples of Norman knights feigning retreat in battles in the 1050s and early 1060s. It seems that William – or maybe some of his knights acting on their own – knew exactly what they were doing.

Harold's death

This was the real turning point. Late in the day, the English army was still holding out against the French attacks. It was the death of King Harold that gave William his victory. The well-known story is that an arrow struck Harold in the eye. Only one source produced within a few years of the battle seems to support this: the Bayeux Tapestry. In the scene below the writing in Latin means 'King Harold is killed'. The image nearby shows an Englishman with an arrow in, or very near, his eye. Is it the King? The problem is that sketches of the tapestry made in the early eighteenth century show the same figure holding a spear that is far longer than this arrow. A nineteenth-century restorer may have turned the spear into an arrow.

The earliest mention of Harold being struck in the eye is in a chronicle from about 1120. Most of the Norman chronicles of the 1070s say nothing about Harold's death. The only one that describes it says that William and a group of knights gathered around the English King and cut him to pieces. One soldier apparently cut Harold in the thigh, although some historians think this is a polite way of saying that he swung his sword into the groin of the English king. Some say the story of the arrow in Harold's eye was invented to hide this more brutal truth.

Whichever version is true, with their king dead, the English finally gave in and tried to flee.

▼ The death of King Harold, from the Bayeux Tapestry, c.1075

> **Reflect**
>
> Why do you think historians cannot agree on one straightforward account of the events described on this page?

What made William a conqueror in 1066?

▲ From the Bayeux Tapestry, c.1075

The end

The final scenes of the Bayeux Tapestry show the Norman cavalry chasing the English off the worn and torn edges of the fabric. It seems appropriate. The English were in disarray. King Harold and his two brothers, Earls Gyrth and Leofwine, as well as thousands of thegns and freemen had died. Thousands more had been killed at Stamford Bridge and Fulford.

The next morning, the Normans buried their dead but they left the English bodies lying above ground. No one is sure what happened to Harold's remains but, years later, William built an abbey whose main altar is said to stand exactly where Harold died. He did this on the orders of the Pope as a way of asking God's forgiveness for all the bloodshed in that place. Over the years a village grew up around the abbey. Its name is, quite simply, Battle.

Record

Complete the notes you have been making on this section (pages 36 to 41).

Remember to use the headings given on page 27.

Review

It is time to decide whether William was, in the words of the historian John Gillingham, 'William the Lucky Bastard'. You should have gathered plenty of evidence to help you make up your mind.

1. Look back through all your notes and consider whether you want to change anything or make any additions now that you know the full story.
2. Then, create your own visual interpretation of what made William a conqueror in 1066. Simply draw four circles like these. Change the sizes of the circles so that the one that you think did most to help William win is the largest. The one that did least is the smallest. Underneath each one, write a brief explanation of why you made it that size.
3. Next, compare your diagram with others in your class. Have they reached the same interpretation as you? Discuss and debate the reasons for any differences.
4. Finally, go back to your diagram and change it if you have been persuaded that there is a better interpretation that fits the evidence. After all, that is one very important way in which interpretations of history develop!

- William's Norman background
- William's personal qualities
- William's opponents' weaknesses and errors
- William's good luck

CLOSER LOOK 2

Battleground

This picture shows tourists visiting the site of the Battle of Hastings – or at least they think they are. In recent years, historians, archaeologists and others have been fighting a battle of their own about exactly where William defeated Harold in 1066.

In 2012, two historians, John Grehan and Martin Mace, published a book arguing that the Battle of Hastings was fought at Caldbec Hill, about one mile away from the traditionally accepted site at the place now known as Battle. They believe that Caldbec fits perfectly the descriptions given in several of the chronicles and that it is strange that no bones of soldiers or remains of weapons have ever been discovered at Battle.

Grehan and Mace called for archaeologists to work on Caldbec Hill, confident that this would reveal the mass burials that took place when the battle ended in 1066.

In 2013, Channel 4's television archaeologists from *Time Team* were given permission to work at both sites. They soon came across a problem at Battle. Since 1966, there has been a re-enactment of the battle each year. The enthusiasts who take part make every effort to wear the right clothing and use the right weapons. Unfortunately, the re-enactments have scattered these modern arrowheads and fragments of swords or chain mail around the site, while tourists leave objects such as ring pulls. These were confusing the *Time Team* metal detectorists until the team used diggers to remove the top few centimetres of soil that was most likely to hold material dropped in recent years.

Battleground

Time Team archaeologists dug three strips totalling about 180 metres across the traditional battlefield and covered a wide area of Caldbec Hill with metal detectors. Neither site produced any finds associated with 1066. They also flew over the whole area with modern equipment that allowed them to work out how different the landscape would have been in the eleventh century. This suggested that William could not have gathered his forces at the bottom of the traditional battle site as the ground was too marshy at that time. Instead, *Time Team* decided, the fighting took place a few hundred yards away where a small roundabout now stands.

The programme entertained millions of viewers and gained a lot of publicity in newspapers. But many professional historians were unimpressed.

In May 2013, historian Marc Morris commented:

> There is sometimes enough evidence to counter the 'make-it-up brigade'. Despite the noisy newspaper headlines in recent months, we can still reasonably suppose that the Battle of Hastings was fought on the site where Battle Abbey now stands because the contemporary sources are so compelling. 'On the very spot where God granted him the conquest of England, William caused a great abbey to be built'. So says the *Anglo-Saxon Chronicle* in a passage clearly composed before 1100 by an Englishman who describes himself as having lived at the king's own court. Unsurprisingly, it is a source that goes unmentioned by those who contend that the battle was fought elsewhere.

3 'Brutal slaughter'

Is this how William gained full control of England, 1067–71?

▲ 'The Conqueror comes to London' by CL Doughty for *Look and Learn* magazine, c.1970. The original caption read 'Arriving at the Saxon city, Duke William marched his army round it, burning and destroying the countryside. Then he built a camp nearby – and settled down to wait.'

Reflect

In this image, the illustrator, Cecil Doughty, has made the Normans look dominant and forceful. How has he done this?

'Brutal slaughter' – Is this how William gained full control of England, 1067–71?

After his victory at Hastings, William rested his troops for two weeks. In that time he hoped that English lords might arrive and surrender the whole kingdom to him. None came. Instead the Witan in London elected young Edgar Atheling as their new king.

William would have to take control of England for himself. He started by ensuring that he controlled the route back to the coast. From the end of October 1066, he marched his army through Kent, building castles in key positions, sometimes being welcomed with gifts by frightened townspeople and sometimes using force to take the supplies his army needed. When William sent an advance party of knights to discover whether London would submit to him, a determined group of Englishmen crossed London Bridge to do battle. The Norman knights easily crushed their resistance but could not take the city. Instead they torched all the houses outside the walls along London's south bank. The illustration on page 44 shows how a children's magazine of the 1970s imagined the scene.

Intimidation and submission

William spent the next weeks marching his army in a wide arc around London. Rather than attack the well-defended burh directly, he had decided to intimidate it into surrender. French chroniclers admit that he used some force as he moved through the countryside, but they try to suggest that William was moderate in his actions. One English chronicler, on the other hand, says he 'laid waste Sussex, Kent, Hampshire, Middlesex and Berkshire'. He then stopped and set up camp, probably at Berkhamsted about thirty miles from London.

Days later, in early December, young Edgar Atheling, or King Edgar as the English would have called him at this stage, rode out to Berkhamsted with a group of leading nobles and clergy. He surrendered the kingdom to William.

> ## Reflect
> What differences can you see between the account given here and the caption that was originally used for the illustration on page 44?

The Enquiry

Illustrators use carefully selected colour, light and shade to create a mood and a message in images like the one on page 44. Historians do the same thing with carefully chosen words. Take the title of this enquiry, for example. We have used it to capture the very complicated story of how King William I established his authority over his newly-won kingdom between 1066 and 1071. It is short and powerful and it carries a particular interpretation of history.

But is it fair? Does it match the evidence available? That is what you will have to decide in this enquiry.

You will learn about:

1. **The first uprisings against Norman rule, 1066–68**
2. **Rebellions in the north, 1068–70**
3. **Rebellion in the east, 1070–71**

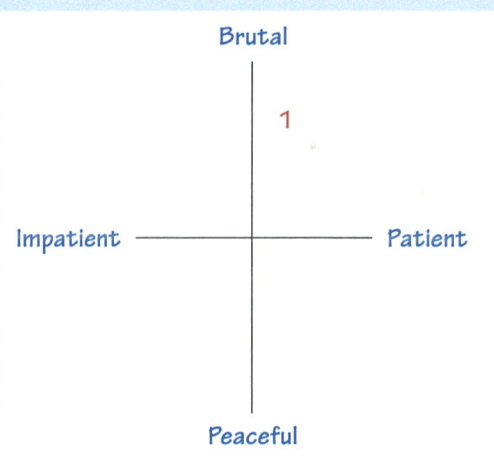

As you work through the enquiry make a timeline of events. It should look like the one below. Write the date and a brief summary of what happened for each event. Then number your events. Then make a large version of the grid on the right. Write each number at the most suitable place. For example, if you believe William's knights' actions near London were fairly brutal but also showed patience by first offering the Londoners a chance to surrender, you could place number 1 at the point shown here.

Date	Event	Number on chart
Nov. 1066	William's knights invited London to submit but burned houses on the south bank when the English refused and fought back.	1

The first uprisings, 1066–68

William wanted to subdue all English resistance before he was officially crowned king. That would allow his wife, Matilda, to be crowned queen alongside him. However, when his English and Norman lords assured him that an early coronation would increase his authority, he agreed to be crowned on Christmas Day 1066 at Westminster Abbey.

London was full of English warriors. Some had arrived there too late to march to Hastings with Harold. Others had taken part in the battle. William was right to feel uneasy. For this reason, he ordered that an armed Norman guard protect the abbey as the coronation service took place.

It was a nervous and tense situation. Inside the abbey, at a critical point in the service, the congregation of several hundred was asked if they would accept William as their king. Chaos followed. This is how the Norman chronicler Orderic Vitalis described the scene:

> At the prompting of the devil, a sudden disaster and portent of future catastrophes occurred. When Archbishop Ealdred asked the English, and Geoffrey Bishop of Coutances asked the Normans, if they would accept William as their king, all of them gladly shouted out with one voice, if not in one language, that they would.
>
> The armed guard outside, hearing the tumult of the joyful crowd in the church and the harsh accents of a foreign tongue, imagined that some treachery was afoot. They rashly set fire to some nearby buildings. The flames spread rapidly from house to house. Throngs of men and women rushed out of the church in frantic haste.
>
> Only the bishops and a few monks remained, terrified, in the abbey. With difficulty they completed the consecration of the king who was trembling from head to foot. The English, after hearing of such misdeeds, never again trusted the Normans who seemed to have betrayed them, but nursed their anger and bided their time to take revenge.

First steps

This uproar in London never became an uprising but it showed how tense the situation was. Anger and resentment filled many of the English while mistrust, anxiety and fear dogged the Normans. Between January and March 1067, William worked to calm the country and establish his authority:

- Edgar, Edwin, Morcar, and other English leaders formally submitted to him.
- William claimed all English lands as his own but allowed earls and thegns to buy their lands back from him. He gave the lands of those who died at Hastings as rewards to those who fought in, or funded, his invasion.
- He led an armed force through East Anglia, knowing that it had strong links with the Danes. He built castles, notably at Norwich where he put his closest friend, William FitzOsbern, in charge of the region.
- He put his half-brother, Odo, Bishop of Bayeux, in charge of the south-east with a base at Dover Castle.

Record

Start your timeline of events and mark your grid as described on page 45.

▲ A life-sized model of William I on his coronation throne, from the Tapestry Museum at Bayeux, France

Reflect

1. The posture, clothing, and expression of museum models give us an interpretation of the person represented.

   What impression of William does this model convey?

2. How does this interpretation compare with the written description of William at his coronation given by Orderic Vitalis?

'Brutal slaughter' – Is this how William gained full control of England, 1067–71?

William returns to Normandy

At the end of March 1067, William felt that England had settled enough for him to return to Normandy. He took with him Edgar Atheling, Earls Edwin and Morcar, and several church leaders. They were kept in comfort, but went as hostages to weaken or discourage any English uprising while he was away. Crowds gathered in Normandy to see William, their conquering hero, the strange long-haired Englishmen beside him and the many fine treasures he had brought back from the English monasteries.

By the spring of 1067, in England, ceorls and thralls were being forced to build motte and bailey castles for their new masters, the Norman knights who had already been granted lands there. William of Poitiers insisted that Odo, FitzOsbern and the knights putting up these castles worked hard to be just and to build up good relations with the English while King William was away. However, Orderic Vitalis, writing later and from the perspective of someone born with an English mother and French father, completely disagreed. He said that the castle owners oppressed the people of their new lands and that Odo and FitzOsbern always sided with the knights if the English complained. William stayed in Normandy and received news of nothing serious enough for him to get involved.

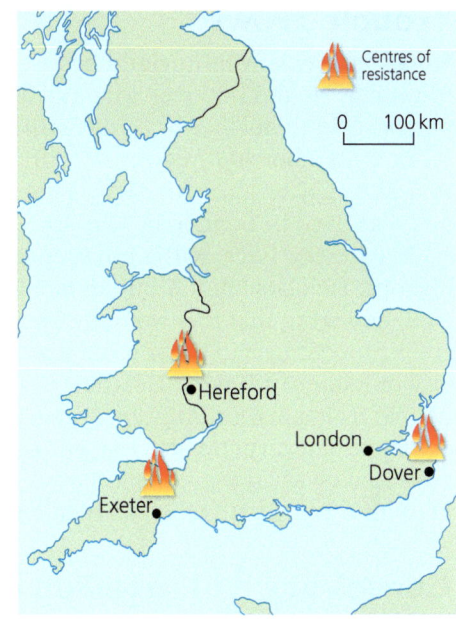

▲ Areas of resistance, 1067 to Easter 1068

The wild man of Mercia

In August 1067, England saw the first of the uprisings shown on this map. It happened around Hereford in the west of the region of Mercia. Its leader was once one of the most powerful English thegns, a man who has become known as Edric the Wild. He had been very wealthy but lost much of his land outside Shropshire to Norman knights after 1066. He joined forces with Welsh princes and raided Norman-held land in Herefordshire, devastating Hereford itself. He gained his name by living in the wild open hills as an outlaw. The Normans used a Latin name for those who hid like this: they were *silvatici* or forest-dwellers.

The rising of August 1067 never really threatened to get out of hand, although Edric continued his raids for years. William saw no need to return from Normandy.

It is not clear what happened to Edric. Like many 'freedom-fighters', legends grew up around him. Stories are told of how he married a fairy queen and still lives in the depths of a lead-mine in Shropshire.

Silent resistance?

The memory of Edric and others who resisted the Normans may also have been kept alive through carvings such as this. A carved head of this type is known as a 'green man'. In the century after 1066, many Norman churches were built all over England. The English stonemasons often decorated the pillars and arches with strange heads that have plants sprouting uncontrollably from their mouths. The tradition pre-dates the Norman Conquest and represents the power of nature and new life. Some historians believe that in the years after the Conquest, the English may have carved them into the Norman churches as an act of silent resistance as these figures were also, like Edric the Wild, called *silvatici*. Much more recently the name 'Wild Edric' has been given to a hiking trail, a garden rose and a locally brewed Shropshire beer. One way or another, Edric's name lives on.

> ### Reflect
> How serious was the uprising in Mercia?

▶ A 'green man' carved on a pillar in Kilpeck Church, Herefordshire, c.1140

Trouble grows

So far, no news from England had worried William enough for him to return. He did not overreact and left his chosen lords, Odo and FitzOsbern, to deal with the difficulties.

In December 1067, however, William's very effective spy network told him that serious trouble was brewing and he left Normandy and was back in London by Christmas.

In January 1068, William met many senior English lords and bishops. He chose not to threaten or accuse them but treated them well, believing that this would be more likely to keep their loyalty. He sent messages to other more distant regions, especially to the city of Exeter in Devon. He knew that its citizens had been calling people from surrounding shires to stand up to the Normans and to come to their city. He also knew that the leader of this determined resistance was Gytha, the mother of King Harold and Earls Leofwine and Gyrth who had died beside their brother at Hastings.

Conspiracy and rebellion in Exeter

Gytha and her daughter had fled to Exeter after William's victory in 1066. Their family had extensive lands in the area. Her local status may explain why so many answered the call to join her in Exeter. In early 1068, they set about repairing and strengthening the burh's defensive walls and towers that were based on the stone defences put up in Roman times.

Gytha had also been plotting with Irish lords. King Harold had three sons by his long-term English mistress, Edith the Fair (or Edith Swan-neck). These young men fled to Ireland where they gathered an invasion force that planned to drive out the Normans. Gytha was also in touch with the Danish king, and hoped that the Danes might invade from the east at the same time.

Negotiation

William had to crush this very threatening power base in Devon. He started by trying to win over Gytha and the leading citizens of Exeter by persuasion. He sent a message urging them to swear an oath of loyalty to him. They replied, refusing the oath, telling him that he would never be allowed in their city and adding that they would not pay a penny more in the tax than they had under English kings. The king sent a message back saying that he could not accept these terms, and gathered an army.

Confrontation

Even though it was mid-winter, in February 1068 William led his army to the south-west in person. It was made up of both Norman and English soldiers. As he neared Exeter, a group of leading citizens came to meet him. They had decided not to defy the King and promised that he could enter the city where his commands would be obeyed. They left some of their group as hostages as a guarantee that they would keep their word.

> **Reflect**
> Which do you think worried William more: events in Kent or events in Northumbria?

▼ Countess Gytha as imagined in a twentieth-century stained-glass window in north Devon. Gytha founded the church in 1053

> **Reflect**
> What impression of Gytha is given in this stained-glass interpretation?

'Brutal slaughter' – Is this how William gained full control of England, 1067–71?

▶ A surviving section of Exeter's city walls. Area 1 dates from Roman times. Area 2 is Anglo-Saxon, when lighter coloured stone from beyond Exeter was used. Area 3 is Norman, but with later medieval repairs. Area 4 is post-medieval

When the rebel spokesman returned to the city, however, their fellow citizens were furious at the deal. William and his army arrived at the city gates to find them firmly closed. The citizens stood on the walls and defied the King.

Seeing that the promise to let him enter had been broken, William brought forward one of the hostages and had his eyes gouged out in full view of Exeter's citizens. This just strengthened their resistance. One, standing high on the wall, bared his bottom and farted loudly in the general direction of King William.

The city surrenders

William's army laid siege to the city. His engineers dug tunnels to undermine its walls. After eighteen days, seeing they could not hold out, the hungry and thirsty citizens surrendered. They sent another delegation to meet the King. Knowing all that had happened since their first group met him, they must have feared the worst. They took with them precious ornaments and holy books and offered them to William as they fell at his feet asking for mercy.

William pardoned them. In return for vows of loyalty he promised that:

- He would not plunder the city.
- He would not punish its people.
- He would not demand extra tax from Exeter.
- He would dispossess Gytha and her daughter of all their family lands and share it among Frenchmen who had supported his invasion. (Gytha and her daughter escaped, either with or without his permission.)

William swore an oath on the holy books they had brought him that he would keep these promises and then allowed the people of Exeter to keep the books and other treasures they had offered. William entered Exeter and posted reliable guards at its gates to stop any looting by less-disciplined soldiers. He chose the highest point in the city and in the spring work began to construct a large motte with a strong fortress on top. Like the old Roman city walls, it was made from the red, volcanic stone of the region and it became known as 'Rougemont' – the red mount. In March 1068, William had got what he wanted: Norman power and even the Norman language was established in the heart of Exeter.

Reflect

1. Why is it significant that William led the army to the south-west in person and that it had both Norman and English soldiers?
2. Why do you think William made his final deal with the rebels of Exeter?

A secure hold on the south-west

After some days, William marched further west, subduing any further resistance in Devon and Cornwall. He ordered that castles be built at key points such as Barnstaple, Totnes, Okehampton and Launceston. By Easter, at the end of March 1068, William was back at Winchester. His campaign to the south-west was over. It looked as though he was gradually establishing his authority, but his most serious challenges lay ahead.

Record

Check that you have clear and helpful points on your timeline up to Easter 1068. Remember to mark each event on your grid to indicate what it reveals about William's treatment of the English. (See page 45.)

Rebellions in the north, 1068–70

The early summer of 1068 showed several signs that England was settling into the pattern that William wanted:

1. William brought Matilda from Normandy to London, showing his confidence that England was safe. On 11 May 1068 she was crowned in Westminster Abbey.
2. Matilda's coronation service was led by the English Archbishop of York, Ealdred. William agreed with the Pope that Stigand, the corrupt Archbishop of Canterbury, was unworthy to lead such an event. But Stigand had sworn loyalty to William so the king let him keep his title despite his obvious faults. William was doing all he could to avoid unnecessary conflict.
3. For the coronation of Matilda, the abbey was filled with both Normans and English lords. William was giving due reward to French lords and knights who served him well but he also preserved the status of those English leaders who stood by him and accepted him as their rightful new king.
4. The document that recorded the coronation and those who witnessed it was specially drawn up in English as well as Latin. William seemed very ready to respect the traditions and identity of his new kingdom.

Reasons to rebel

Despite these appearances, there were problems below the surface. At William's coronation in 1066, the tension, fear and distrust had spilled out for all to see. At Matilda's coronation in 1068, they were still there along with growing resentment on the part of the English, but they were all well hidden ... at least for the time being.

There were many reasons why the English might break into open rebellion against the Normans:

> **Record**
>
> Start the next section of your timeline and mark your grid as described on page 45.

▲ The head of Queen Matilda, from a nineteenth century statue in Paris. We have no clear idea of what she actually looked like, but we do know that she and William were devoted to each other

> **Reflect**
>
> From the list given at the start of this page, what do you think William wanted his 'pattern' for England to be?

1. **Revenge**. Some, such as Gytha, the mother of King Harold, were desperate to avenge loved ones lost in battle at Hastings.
2. **Pride**. Others hated having foreigners ruling over them. There were regular attacks on Normans if they dared to walk or ride alone at night.
3. **Dispossession**. Loss of land was a powerful motive. Some had lost their right to the family land if their father or husband had died fighting the Normans. Others who had rebelled and survived lost their land as a punishment.
4. **Disrespect for new lords**. French lords who took over land from English thegns often did not know or follow English ways so were not respected.
5. **Taxation**. William imposed two heavy tax demands on the English in his first two years as king.
6. **Loss of status**. Earls such as Edwin and Morcar retained their titles, but lost large parts of their land to Norman knights or favoured Englishmen, therefore reducing their status.
7. **Distance**. The fringes of the country were far harder to control than the south-east. People in the north and west were less aware of the Norman takeover at first but when it did hit them they reacted with anger.
8. **Numbers**. The English far outnumbered their new Norman masters.

'Brutal slaughter' – Is this how William gained full control of England, 1067–71?

William rides north (1) – summer 1068

In summer 1068, not many weeks after Matilda's coronation, William received a strange message. It was a declaration from the people of the north of England to say that they would stand and fight him if he should ever set foot on their lands. The north-east had always felt independent from the rest of England, but this was too much. William had to act. He gathered an army and marched north.

The bold declaration to the King followed an agreement reached between Earls Edwin and Morcar, Edgar Atheling and various lords in the north and on borders with Wales. They had all decided to stand up to William. Their motives included most of those listed on page 50, but there was an extra factor. William promised to give his daughter to Earl Edwin as a wife. By spring 1068, it was obvious that the promise would not be kept. This may have been the final straw. Ealdred, Archbishop of York, tried to persuade the rebels to hold back, but the message was sent.

Castle power

William marched from Winchester directly into the heart of Earl Edwin's lands in Mercia. At Warwick he immediately set about building a motte and bailey castle. The best site was occupied by houses that belonged to the Abbot of Coventry but he simply tore these down and set local people to work making the huge earth mound on which a powerful timber stockade was then built. This was a pattern that became familiar all over England.

The *Anglo-Saxon Chronicle* says that William 'allowed his men to harry wherever they came' on this campaign. This means they could attack with determination and persistence. It seems that William was not using the tactics he had employed earlier at Exeter in the spring.

On reaching Nottingham, William built another castle. By then, word had reached Edwin and Morcar that the king was using his power to great effect and they chose to surrender to him. William showed them mercy. He allowed them to live and to keep their titles, but their actual power shrank still further.

The king pressed on northwards to York, the capital of the north of England. By the time he arrived, around July 1068, the rebels had fled. Another castle went up. William stayed to ensure all was well before he marched south again, building three more castles at Lincoln, Huntingdon and Cambridge as he went.

▲ Areas of resistance, June 1068 to September 1068

Reflect

Why do you think William built all these castles further south when the problem he faced was in the far north?

The defeat of Harold's sons

William must have felt the country was being stabilised, especially as he received some more positive news. In June or July, when William was in the north, Harold's sons had sailed with a considerable armed force from Ireland. They had urged the people of Bristol to let them set up a base there, but the people took up arms and fought them off. If the English were prepared to drive away the sons of their former king in order to keep William in control, he must have been very encouraged indeed.

▲ 'Clifford's Tower' in York standing on the motte (mound) where William built his castle in 1068. It commands two river crossings. The stone tower was built in the thirteenth century

▲ Areas of resistance, January 1069 to September 1069

William rides north (2) – spring 1069

After the rising of 1068, William made Robert of Comines the new Earl of northern Northumbria. Three different English lords had held the position in the previous two years and none had kept the peace. William was turning to a foreign professional soldier to do the job. Robert brought with him over five hundred armed mercenaries.

At the end of January 1069, Robert led a heavy-handed attack on rebels at Durham. He and his army forced their way into the town and began looting and killing. The people of Durham fought back, cutting down the soldiers in the streets and setting fire to the house where Robert and the rest of his men had taken refuge. They all died.

The killing at Durham sparked another general rising in the north. Edgar Atheling and the rebel leaders reappeared from Scotland. Once again they attacked York. William's men there sent word to the King and he set off at speed to deal with his second crisis in the region.

William did not stop to build castles this time. His massive army caught the rebels by surprise and, in a bloody battle, they regained the city. Once again the leaders escaped and Edgar reached safety in Scotland. The king built a second castle and left the city in the hands of his most trusted friend and highly experienced soldier, William FitzOsbern. He must have thought it would now be secure at last.

Invasion in Devon – June 1069

By mid-April, the king was back at Winchester with Matilda, but during the summer the trouble continued in the north and he sent her back to Normandy. There was real danger when Harold's sons sailed again from Ireland, this time with a fleet of over sixty ships and a large army. Brian of Brittany, who was William's commander in the south-west, marched an army to north Devon and fought the invaders, probably near the coastal village of Appledore. About 1,700 men died in the battle. Harold's sons were once again driven off.

Invasion in Yorkshire – September 1069

In early September 1069, a fleet of over 250 ships gathered off the coast of Yorkshire, having first raided the south-east coast. The Danes had returned.

Gytha, the mother of King Harold, went to Denmark after the failure of her grandsons' invasion of north Devon. She may have persuaded the Danish king, Svein II, that he could win the English crown by sending a large army to join the rebels in the north of England.

For whatever reason, Svein sent his brother, Asbjørn, across the sea with an enormous army. He landed in the Humber estuary and met the rebel force, once again led by Edgar Atheling. They headed directly for York.

On hearing the news, Ealdred, Archbishop of York, died of shock. He had been one of the few English leaders who encouraged the English to keep the peace. There was little peace in England for the next four months.

> **Reflect**
> The artist shows Ealdred as a saintly man, dying at a moment of high drama. How has he done this?

▲ Archbishop Ealdred dies on hearing that the Danes were about to attack York. From *The Story of the British Nation*, 1920

52

William rides north (3) – winter 1069

The joint force of English rebels and Danish invaders reached York on 20 September. They arrived to find it in flames. The citizens had feared that their enemies might use timbers from houses near the castles to bridge the moat. Their solution was to set fire to them, but the fire got out of control and destroyed their already much-battered city. The rebels and the Danes therefore plundered what they could and withdrew into the marshes of north Lincolnshire.

For the third time in just over a year, William gathered an army and marched north to deal with a crisis. This time he started from Gloucestershire where he had been hunting. He made his way into Lincolnshire and did what he could to defeat the rebels and Danes, but they were carefully avoiding any pitched battle by spreading around the marshlands.

The flames spread

While he was there, William learned that rebels in the west, including Edric the Wild, who had never been captured, had taken the opportunity offered by the Danish threat to revive full-scale attacks along the Welsh borders. Edric and his *silvatici*, or 'untameable Englishmen' as Orderic Vitalis called them, besieged Shrewsbury, burned it to the ground and ran into hiding when a Norman army came to meet them. At about the same time, trouble flared again in the south-west. Men from Cornwall and Devon attacked Exeter, while others from Dorset and Somerset besieged Montacute Castle. Interestingly, the people of Exeter stayed loyal to William this time and held out against the rebels there.

William ordered another Norman army to move into the south-west while he marched his own force from Lincolnshire to Stafford, where another rebellion had broken out. He put down the revolt but it was a bloody business.

William's three-part plan

The King had to find a way to stop these constant risings in the north, as they opened the way for more rebellions elsewhere.

On hearing that the Danes had re-assembled in York, he turned his army around and headed back north. He was delayed on the way as an important bridge had been destroyed. By the time he reached York in early December, the Danes and rebels had once again drifted away into hiding. William feared that they wanted to live off the land and the local farms over the winter and await the arrival of more men from Denmark in the spring.

The King knew that he would have to do something that would have a lasting effect in the north: he

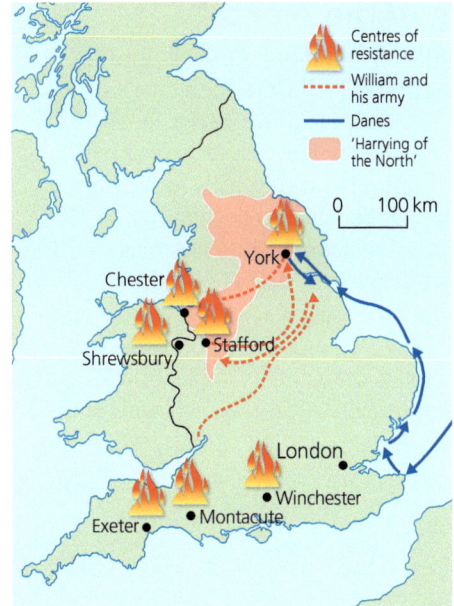

▲ Areas of resistance, September 1069 to March 1070

could not keep marching armies up to York to subdue rebellions in the region.

His first action was to order that the two castles be rebuilt but he needed more than this. He came up with a three-part plan. He would:

1. **Pay the Danes huge sums of money to leave.** This had worked before in England and elsewhere.
2. **Send for his coronation crown.** William knew that wearing the crown on Christmas Day in the city's battered Minster (church) would remind his subjects that he was God's chosen king.
3. **Destroy the land.** He had reached a point where he was ready to inflict massive destruction on vast areas of the north so that no enemy army could live there. But nor could its people.

The Danes accepted their bribe and returned to their ships. The Christmas ceremony went ahead. Then William rode to Chester to crush the latest rising there, although his army almost mutinied when faced with marching again across rough paths in icy weather. Other troops were spread widely and told to find and kill any remaining rebels, and to carry out what has become known as the 'Harrying of the North'.

Reflect
Which part of William's plan makes most sense to you?

The 'Harrying of the North'

The half-Norman, half-English monk Orderic Vitalis described what happened as William's men carried out the third part of his plan. He described how, from January to March 1070, they worked their way across more than a hundred miles of land in hills and valleys, tracking down and killing rebels and destroying any place where they may have been hiding. Historians think they covered the shaded area on the map on page 53.

All this killing was deeply unpleasant but although Orderic shows concern at the amount of blood shed, he seems to see it is a part of the grim realities of war at the time. Here is how he describes what really troubled him:

> In his anger the king commanded that all crops, herds, farming tools and food of every kind should be collected and burned to ashes in consuming fire, so that the whole region north of the river Humber should be stripped of all means of sustenance … As a consequence, so terrible a famine fell on the humble and defenceless people, that more than 100,000 Christians of both sexes, young and old, perished of hunger.
>
> I have frequently praised William, but for this act that condemned the innocent and guilty alike to die by slow starvation I cannot.
>
> When I think of helpless children, young men in the prime of life and white-bearded old men perishing alike of hunger, I am moved to pity. I would rather lament the grief and sufferings of the wretched people than make a vain attempt to flatter the man responsible for such dreadful deeds.
>
> Such brutal slaughter cannot remain unpunished … The almighty judge will weigh the deeds of men.

'Brutal slaughter' – is this how William gained full control of England, 1067–71?

Some historians believe the range and impact of the 'Harrying of the North' has been exaggerated:

An extract from 'Feudal politics in Yorkshire' by historian Paul Dalton, 1990

Despite the neatness of the theory there are logical grounds for … disposing of the myth that the Conqueror organized a systematic devastation of the north. Although the graphic accounts of several chroniclers leave little doubt that there was major destruction of some kind … it is questionable whether William had the manpower and time necessary to reduce vast areas of a county the size of Yorkshire to a depopulated, uncultivated desert. In the late 1060s the bulk of his troops must surely have been stationed in the castles that were under construction everywhere in the south of England and Welsh Marches, and his visit to Yorkshire in 1069–1070 lasted no more than three months and may have been considerably shorter.

An alternative interpretation is given in these words used in a television documentary about the 'Harrying of the North':

An extract from the script of *The Normans*, a BBC television series, 2010. It is written by the historian Robert Bartlett

The Normans devastated the north of England. They sacked every village and farmstead as they went. Then William divided his troops into smaller bands who destroyed any crops and livestock they could find.

Those who survived were reduced to eating horses, dogs, cats – some say, even human flesh. A stream of refugees began pouring south. [A monk] tells of a huge crowd of old men, young men, women with infants fleeing the misery of the famine.

A huge area across northern and central England was laid waste by this 'scorched earth' on the northern rebels. Plotting the settlements destroyed by the Normans shows the scar that was carved across the country by William's army. Sixteen years later, [when the Domesday Book was compiled] these areas were still desolate wasteland.

Reflect

You may have noticed that we have taken the title of this enquiry from the words of Orderic Vitalis on page 54.

1. Find where he uses the phrase 'brutal slaughter'.
2. What aspect of William's behaviour does Orderic Vitalis pick out for his most severe criticism?
3. How and why do the two historians differ in their interpretations of the 'Harrying of the North'?
4. These pages are another way of interpreting the 'Harrying of the North'. Why do you think we chose to design them as we have?

Record

Check that you have a clear and helpful set of notes in your timeline up to March 1070, after the Harrying of the North. Remember to mark each event on your grid to indicate what it reveals about William's treatment of the English. (See page 45.)

Rebellion in the east, 1070–71

At Christmas 1069, William had been in York and was just embarking on the 'Harrying of the North'. By the end of March 1070, he had subdued Chester and was back in London. The work of 'harrying' was probably ending by then, although its effects were felt for many years after. When William made his famous Domesday survey of landholding in 1085, the records showed large areas in the north were still depopulated.

At Easter 1070, William had his second coronation at Westminster Abbey. The Pope had sent two cardinals (leading churchmen) to England. They crowned the king and publicly showed the Pope's blessing for the conquest of England. But there was a price to pay for the victory and for the bloodshed that had followed.

The Church and warfare

The Roman Catholic Church taught that souls go to heaven more speedily and with less pain if people do penance (voluntary suffering) for their sins before they die. The Church taught that killing in war was sinful. The penance for soldiers varied according to how many people they had killed. In William's case, having killed an unknown number, he would have to do penance for a day a week until he died. There was an alternative though: he could pay for a new church to be built. Sometime around 1070, William ordered the building of Battle Abbey on the site of the Battle of Hastings. It was only completed in 1094 after William's death. Other knights did something similar by paying sums of money to existing monasteries or building fine stone churches on their new lands.

Church resistance and Church reform

William worked with the Pope's cardinals to make important changes to the Church from 1070. They were certainly designed to improve the quality of the Church in England but the King was using the cardinals to help him tighten his political control and end resistance. Some of the main changes around Easter 1070 were:

1. Stigand was finally replaced as Archbishop of Canterbury. He had never been directly involved in encouraging rebellion, but he was a corrupt and unhelpful reminder of the days before the conquest. The new archbishop was Lanfranc, an Italian priest who had served for many years in Norman monasteries.

> **Record**
> Start the next section of your timeline and mark your grid as described on page 45.

▲ A reconstruction by artist Peter Urmston, showing how the interior of Battle Abbey may have looked when it opened in 1094. Drawn c.2010

2. Other senior Church leaders were replaced by Norman priests and monks. Most of those who lost their posts had shown support or sympathy for the rebels. The King imprisoned some for life. Just as William had lost patience with English thegns and earls and had passed their lands to Normans, so he had decided that churchmen must also be brought into line.

3. William ordered all monasteries to provide men (or money instead) to serve the king as knights. This was common practice in Normandy and elsewhere in Europe, but it had never been done in the English Church. After so much stubborn resistance from his English subjects, William was moving away from his earlier promise to respect English traditions.

> **Reflect**
> Do you think these reforms of the Church would have done more to help or to hinder William as he tried to end resistance in England?

'Brutal slaughter' – Is this how William gained full control of England, 1067–71?

Hereward and resistance at Ely

Dealing with uprisings was expensive, both in cash and in soldiers' lives. That is why William ordered monasteries to provide soldiers. That same spring, the King found another way to raise funds. He discovered that many wealthy Englishmen were hiding their personal treasure in monasteries, as these were safer than their own houses. William ordered a search of all monasteries and took away all such hidden wealth and many of the monasteries' treasures as well. It upset many Church leaders, but it meant that he had the funds he needed to pay off his mercenaries and send them home. He was confident that the country was peaceful again.

Just a few weeks later, a final uprising burst into life. This time the trouble was in East Anglia and it centred on the abbey at Ely.

Fens and Danes

In the eleventh century, Ely was an island that stood just a few metres above the East Anglian marshland that was called the Fens. A small town had built up on the island around an abbey. In June 1070, the island was suddenly overrun by an army of Danes. These were the same men who had promised William at Christmas that they would return to their homeland. They had not. Their leader was still Asbjørn, the brother of the Danish king. In May, King Svein himself had arrived with reinforcements, and they now struck deep into the Fens, taking the town and abbey of Ely with no resistance. The English in the area cheered them on. They hoped and believed that the Danes had come to remove King William.

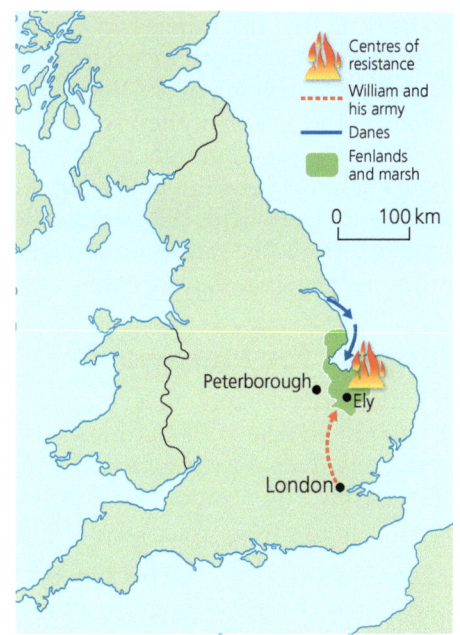

▲ Areas of resistance, 1070–71

◀ A British Railways poster, c.1955. It uses an image of Hereward to encourage tourists to visit Ely by train

Hereward

On 2 June 1070, just after the Danes took Ely, an English thegn called Hereward carried out a raid on a different abbey. This one was at Peterborough, about 30 miles away. Hereward led a large group of armed warriors into the town and burned most of its houses before breaking into the abbey and stealing all its gold, silver and jewellery. He planned this raid when he heard that Peterborough was to get a new Norman abbot. He thought the English should have the valuables rather than William's French priests.

Having taken the treasures, Hereward presented them to the Danes to thank them for fighting the Normans. He was an outlaw who had a large following. He had already led many successful attacks against the Normans in East Anglia and Lincolnshire. He joined forces with the Danes and they created a strong, well-protected base on the island of Ely from where they could defy the power of the Normans in and around the Fens.

> ### Reflect
> The poster makes Hereward seem brave and defiant. How does it do this?

The Danes depart

On hearing that the Danes had taken Ely, William acted quickly. He arranged to meet King Svein and they agreed that he and his Danish armies would sail home. The 'Harrying of the North' meant that the men who had spent the winter in the mouth of the River Humber had struggled to feed themselves. Svein knew they would not be able to fight well. His own reinforcements alone could not take England from William. Just a few weeks after joining forces with Hereward, the Danes sailed back to Denmark, taking the treasures from Ely and Peterborough with them. Hereward was left to fend for himself against the Normans.

Support for Hereward

William seemed happy to let his local knights and the new Abbot of Peterborough deal with Hereward once the Danes had left. He sailed back to Normandy to deal with some matters there. By the time the King returned in 1071, Hereward's position had strengthened. There were several reasons for this:

1. The Abbot of Ely gave his support to Hereward using the island as a base.
2. An English bishop joined Hereward's force and brought with him rebels who had escaped from the north.
3. Edwin and Morcar left William's court. After failing to start a new rising on their own, they decided to join Hereward. Some sources say that only Morcar reached Ely and Edwin died on the way.
4. Warriors from across England made their way to Ely when it became known that another rising was under way. Hereward's army grew.

At some point in 1071, probably in the spring, William decided that the rising in Ely was too serious to be left to the local lords to sort out. Yet again he gathered an army and marched to East Anglia.

The siege of Ely

The King could not rely on brute force to end this rising. He sent ships to block supplies and prevent them reaching Ely from the sea, and boats to cut off access to and from the east of the Fens. To the west, William's soldiers started to build a causeway through the marshland. Over the deeper sections, it had timber bridges that more or less floated on the water.

Hereward and his men managed to defend their base for some time. The sources for Hereward's life are filled with improbable, heroic stories. In one of these, William recruited a local witch and built a high wooden tower from which she could curse the rebels across the marshes. Her curses involved baring her bottom and farting at them. Hereward's heroic response was to work his way across the marsh and, with a burning torch, he set fire to the reeds and the platform so that the witch was burned.

Part of the story, at least, is suggested on the tourist poster on page 57.

> ## Reflect
> Why do you think William eventually chose to get personally involved in defeating the uprising at Ely?

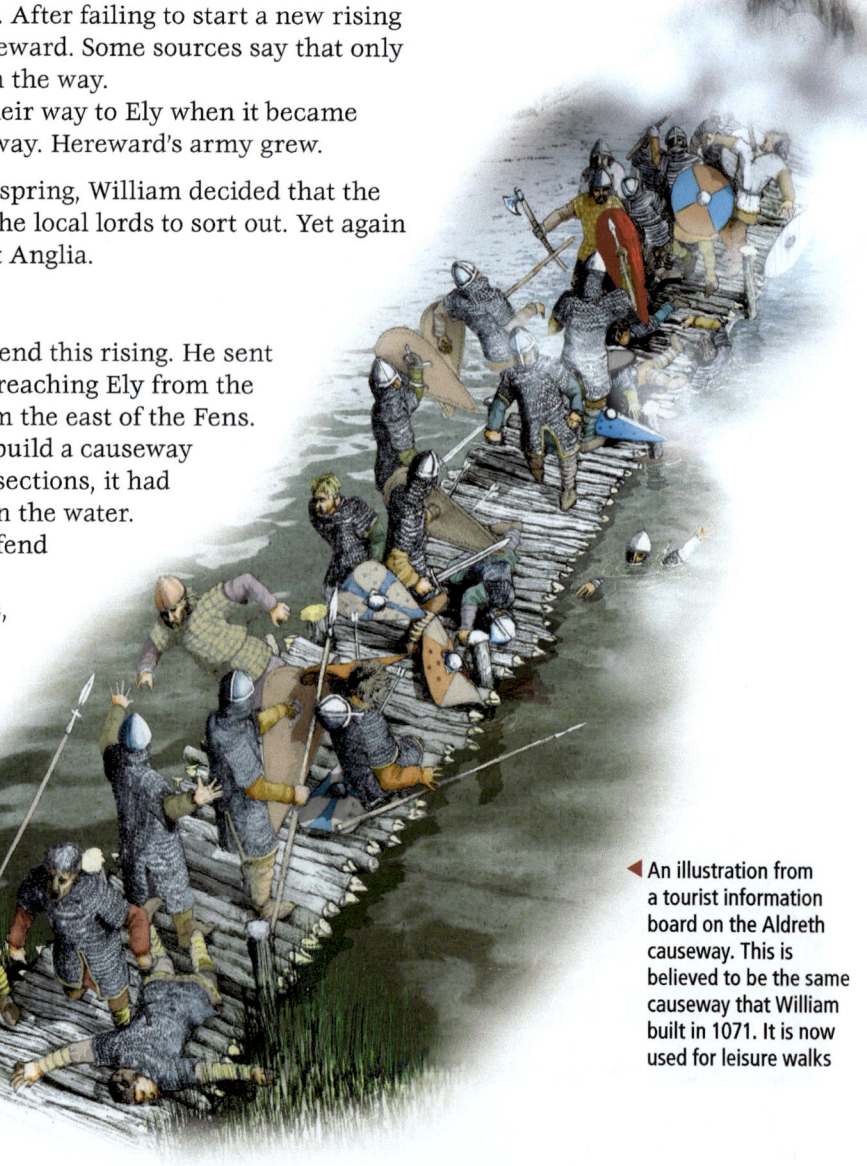

◀ An illustration from a tourist information board on the Aldreth causeway. This is believed to be the same causeway that William built in 1071. It is now used for leisure walks

'Brutal slaughter' – Is this how William gained full control of England, 1067–71?

William's victory

In the end, William's army reached the island. They either marched across the newly built causeway or, according to some sources, monks from the abbey, hoping to win the King's favour, betrayed the rebels and led them over another secret pathway. The English surrendered. Morcar and other leaders were imprisoned. Other rebels had their hands cut off or eyes gouged out.

Hereward escaped. He continued his resistance but never posed the same threat to the King. The rising at Ely in 1070–71 proved to be the last widespread and serious uprising that William had to face.

We have no clear idea what happened to Hereward. Just like Edric the Wild he became a hero of English legends. In Victorian times he became known as 'The last of the English'.

Review

This enquiry is an interpretation of history and we chose to call it 'Brutal slaughter'. Use your timeline of events between 1066 and 1071 and your grid to decide whether you think it should be given a different title.

Write an essay that answers this question:

It is fair to say that King William I ended resistance in England by a policy of 'bloody slaughter'.

If you want to disagree with the statement, end your essay with an alternative title for the enquiry.

Record

Check that you have a clear and helpful set of notes on your timeline up to the end of the resistance at Ely in 1071. Remember to mark each event on your grid to indicate what it reveals about William's treatment of the English. (See page 45.)

▼ A recent photograph of Ely across the Fens. The cathedral was built by the Normans on the site where the much smaller abbey once stood

CLOSER LOOK 3

Hereward the Wake – the last of the English

▲ 'Hereward the Wake', an engraving by H.C. Selous, 1870

This picture illustrates a scene from the novel *Hereward the Wake – The last of the English*, by Charles Kingsley.

On returning to England after years away, the hero, an exiled English thegn called Hereward, goes to his family's home at Bourne in Lincolnshire. In the years since he was last there, the Normans had invaded and shortly before his return some French knights had taken the family lands, murdered Hereward's brother and had nailed his head above the door of his house. Hereward sees his brother's head and, in his fury, finds the Normans who are all together eating and drinking. He bursts in on them and mercilessly hacks them down in their drunken and unarmed state. He cuts them up and nails the fifteen Norman heads over the doorway for all to see. From that moment, Hereward becomes the freedom-fighter who leads the English resistance in the Fens against William the Conqueror.

Hereward the Wake – the last of the English

The author and the artist

This all sounds like a scene from a violent X-rated action film in our own day. In fact, the novel was written in 1865 by Charles Kingsley, who was both a priest and a professor of history at the University of Cambridge. The engraving was made in 1870. In the five years after the novel was published, it became a bestseller and a notable artist, H.C. Selous, produced a whole series of engravings showing key scenes from the book.

The mood of the time

The novel and the images caught the mood of the time. Nineteenth-century public opinion in England was largely anti-French. This stemmed from the start of the century when Britain was at war with France. The British saw the French emperor, Napoleon, as a dictator who forced his will on the nations he conquered all across Europe. At one point Napoleon seemed sure to invade Britain and he was confident of success. He brought the Bayeux Tapestry out for a public viewing to remind the French that they had successfully invaded Britain in 1066 and could do it again in his own day. That invasion never came, but the British were slow to forgive and forget his behaviour.

In the late nineteenth century, the British felt much closer to Germany. Queen Victoria had married a German prince, Albert of Saxe-Coburg Gotha. Historians such as Kingsley reminded the British that the Anglo-Saxons first came to England from Germany and argued that they brought with them the early forms of democracy that had helped to give Britain the freedom that they were so proud of. The Oxford historian E.A. Freeman wrote a fifteen volume *History of the Norman Conquest* that argued that the Normans took away many of those ancient freedoms and that it had taken 'the English' centuries to win them back. That history book appeared in 1867, just after Kingsley's novel was published.

Other historians disagreed, but it was Kingsley's and Freeman's interpretation that won public acceptance. The influence of their ideas is still strong.

▲ Charles Kingsley. A nineteenth century engraving

Kingsley's views

Kingsley particularly admired the strength and courage of the Vikings who had settled in the northern and eastern counties of England, the area known as Danelaw. He believed they gave extra qualities to English life when blended with Anglo-Saxon culture. His hero, Hereward, was descended from them. This extract from the opening pages of Kingsley's novel reminds readers of what happened to England between 1066 and 1072. It shows his point of view very clearly:

> When the men of Wessex, the once conquering, and … most civilized, race of Britain, fell at Hastings once and for all, and struck no second blow, then the men of the Danelaw disdained to yield to the Norman invader.
>
> For seven long years they held their own, not knowing, like true Englishmen, when they were beaten; and fought on desperate, till there were none left to fight. Their bones lay white on every island in the fens; their corpses rotted on gallows beneath every Norman keep; their few survivors crawled into monasteries, with eyes picked out, hands and feet cut off; or took to the wild wood as strong outlaws, like their successor Robin Hood, but they never really bent their necks to the Norman yoke: they kept alive in their hearts that proud spirit of personal independence, which they brought with them from the moors of Denmark and the dales of Norway; and they kept alive, too, those free institutions which were without a doubt the germs [seeds] of our British Liberty.

4 Military fortresses or status symbols?

What can research reveal about early Norman castles?

The image below was produced in the 1970s by Ron Embleton, a children's book illustrator. He imagined a scene in an Anglo-Saxon village at the time of the Norman Conquest.

In the foreground of the picture, a peasant family is hard at work. One woman is feeding hens. Another is carrying water to the house, helped by a young boy. A man is busy splitting a large tree trunk. He looks up as a neighbour waves to him, but he does not stop his work.

In the background, Ron Embleton included a Norman castle. As you can see, the castle is made entirely of timber. A wooden tower, surrounded by a palisade, sits on top of a huge mound of earth known as a motte. At the base of the motte is the bailey, a larger area containing various wooden buildings. The bailey is surrounded by a palisade and a wide ditch. A wooden bridge spans the ditch, and steep wooden steps connect the bailey to the motte.

In the two decades after 1066, the Normans built hundreds of these motte and bailey castles, mostly using Anglo-Saxon labour. It is hard to imagine what the Anglo-Saxons must have felt as they looked up at these strange new buildings which so clearly demonstrated the power of their new masters. Ron Embleton's sympathy seems to have been with the Saxon man forced to work the timber for the new castle. He included a dark sky behind the Norman castle to suggest that this was a building which brought trouble and menace to the lives of the Saxons.

What can research reveal about early Norman castles?

There is probably a Norman castle close to where you live. If it was an important castle it might have been re-built in stone and it will now be much bigger than it was in early Norman times. Maybe it has become a tourist attraction. More likely though, your nearest Norman castle will have been abandoned at some point in the Middle Ages. It will probably have left little trace because the timber structures have rotted away. Bumps in the ground known as 'earthworks' may be the only clues as to what the castle looked like. This is why illustrators like Ron Embleton have to use a mixture of evidence and imagination in their work.

The Enquiry

The story of early Norman castles is usually told in a simple and straightforward way.

- Children's history books and websites often begin the story of English castles in 1066.
- Pictures like the one painted by Ron Embleton can give the impression that all early Norman castles looked alike.
- Popular history books frequently only portray castles as military fortresses which were used in the brutal conquest of England after 1066.

Historians and archaeologists try to uncover a more complex and interesting story of early Norman castles.

In this enquiry, you will decide what their research can reveal to answer the following three questions:

1. What was new about Norman castles in England?
2. Where did the Normans build castles and what did their castles look like?
3. What exactly were Norman castles for?

At the end of the enquiry you will use your knowledge to design some web pages which improve the simple story of Norman castles found on an educational website.

◀ A Saxon village with a motte and bailey castle in the background, by the children's illustrator Ron Embleton, c.1970

What was new about Norman castles in England?

In the two centuries before the Norman Conquest, the Anglo-Saxons had built many fortified sites in England. As you discovered in Enquiry 1, Anglo-Saxon kings had built defended towns known as burhs across England. These walled towns were centres of royal administration, and their defences provided the Saxons with protection in case of Viking attack. The royal burhs of the Saxon kings are often mentioned in history books, but less well-known are the smaller defended sites built by thegns. These are known as burh-geats.

The burh-geats of Saxon thegns

Archaeological digs can reveal some interesting features of Anglo-Saxon burh-geats. At Goltho, in Lincolnshire, archaeologists uncovered an egg-shaped enclosure about the size of a football pitch. This contained the thegn's hall where he feasted with his followers, a separate kitchen and buildings where the thegn and his family slept.

Surrounding the enclosure was a two-metre-deep ditch and a two-metre-high earth bank. Archaeologists think that there was a wooden palisade on top of the earth bank which may have added another two metres to the height of the defences. A cross-section of the defences is shown on this reconstruction drawing which is carefully based on the archaeological evidence.

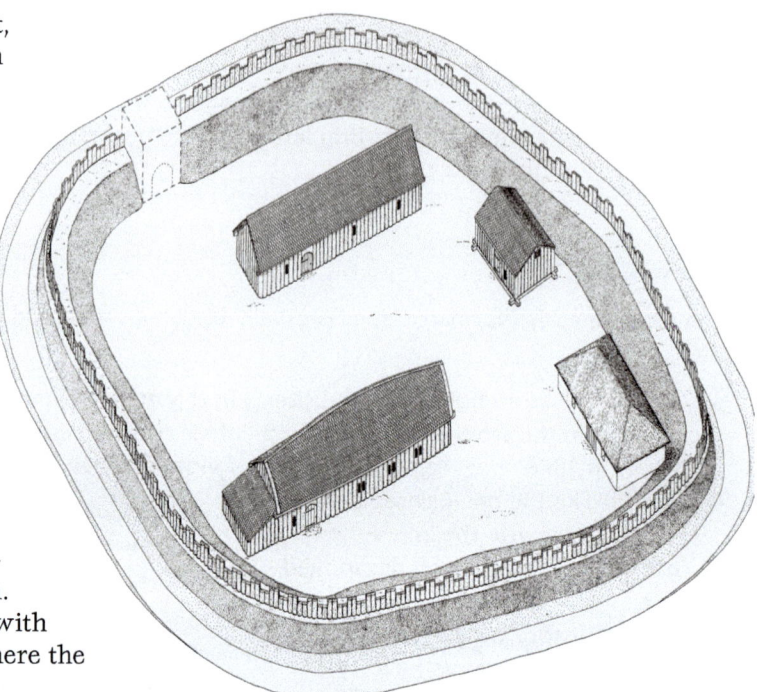

▲ A reconstruction of the late Anglo-Saxon burh-geat at Goltho, near Lincoln

> **Reflect**
> 1. Which building do you think was the thegn's hall?
> 2. How was the site defended?

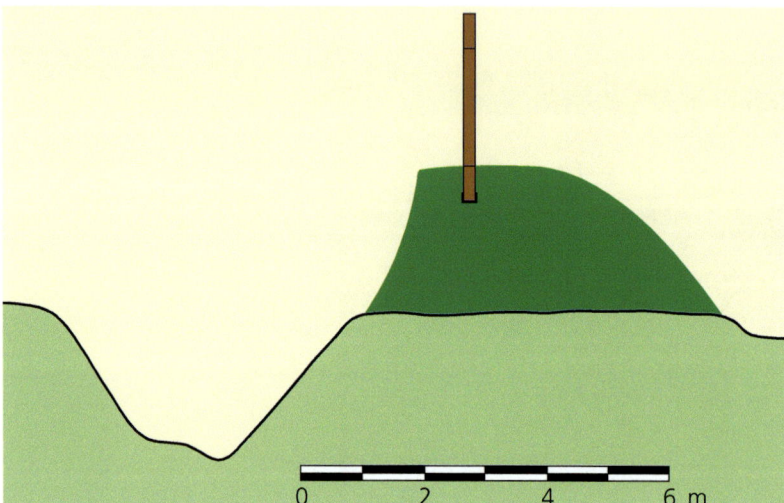

▲ A cross-section of the defences at Goltho in the early eleventh century

> **Reflect**
> Think about the size of these defences in relation to your classroom. How much protection did they provide?

It is possible that many Anglo-Saxon thegns lived in fortified enclosures surrounded by massive banks and ditches. Other archaeological digs have shown that these often contained an impressive multi-storeyed gatehouse at the entrance. Some archaeologists think that the defended homes of Saxon thegns may have been more about showing off than defence. They argue that burh-geats were impressive features in the landscape which were intended to show the status of their owners. Certainly, nobody in Anglo-Saxon England ever named these defended sites 'castles'. The word 'castle' was first used to describe a completely new fortification which was brought to England by the Normans in the 1050s – a 'motte'.

What can research reveal about early Norman castles?

The first mottes in England and Wales

In 1051, a monk from Peterborough Abbey complained in the *Anglo-Saxon Chronicle* that some Norman friends of King Edward the Confessor had arrived in England and were causing trouble in Herefordshire near the border with Wales. The monk was surprised by the new buildings that the Normans had built. These were huge mounds of earth topped with wooden towers and surrounded by a wooden palisade. There was no English word to describe the new buildings, so the monk used a foreign word – *castle*.

The three mottes built in Herefordshire during the 1050s were the earliest castles in England. They were built to help Edward the Confessor in his power struggle with Earl Godwin. No one could have guessed at the time that in the two decades after 1066 England would be filled with hundreds of these Norman castles.

Castles in France

In France, the word 'castle' was used almost two hundred years earlier than it was in England. By the eleventh century, the Normans had adopted many French ideas about warfare and defence. In particular, they had begun to fight on horseback and to build castles in their province of Normandy.

In the Bayeux Tapestry we find some clues about what these castles from the early eleventh century might have looked like. However, the evidence is difficult to interpret. This picture of the castle at Dinan shows knights defending the castle against attackers. Some of the attackers are on horseback, while others are trying to set fire to the castle with burning torches.

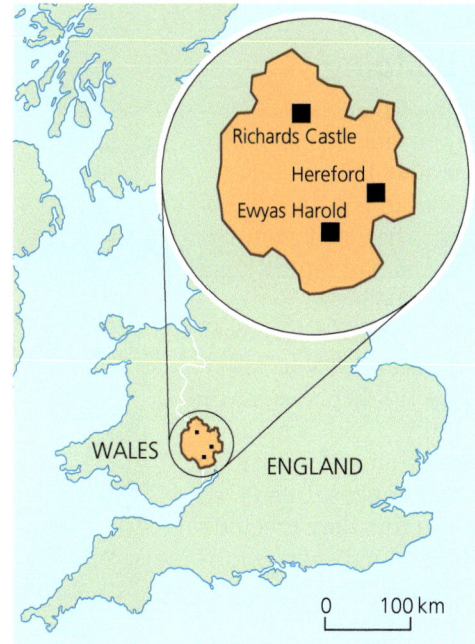

▲ A map showing the earliest castles in England

Reflect

What can the picture tell us about the following features:

- the motte
- the palisade
- the tower
- the bridge
- the entrance
- the bailey?

▼ The castle at Dinan, from the Bayeux Tapestry

Invasion and castle-building

When William Duke of Normandy invaded England in September 1066 he made the wise decision to land at Pevensey. In the third century AD the Romans had built a huge fort here. By 1066, the fort at Pevensey was in ruins, but the massive walls and towers still provided useful defences for the Norman army. The Normans quickly set about strengthening the Roman defences. In one corner of the fort they erected an earth bank and palisade to create a smaller, but stronger, fortress. This picture by the reconstruction artist Alan Sorrell imagines what the Norman castle at Pevensey may have looked like soon after the Normans landed.

▲ A painting of the Norman castle at Pevensey in 1066, by the reconstruction artist Alan Sorrell

Reflect

Alan Sorrell's illustration helps us to picture the site at Pevensey in the autumn of 1066. What interesting details did he include?

Hastings Castle

The Normans soon built another castle further along the coast at Hastings. They used the same approach that they had adopted at Pevensey, creating a strongly defended site in the corner of an Iron Age fort. This time, however, the Normans seem to have built a motte. The picture below, from the Bayeux Tapestry, gives us some clues about what the castle at Hastings looked like and how it was built. However, the picture leaves many questions unanswered.

There seems to be a timber palisade on top of the motte, but was there also a tower inside the palisade?

The five men building the motte seem to be using picks and shovels. How many men were really needed to build a motte, and how long would it have taken them? Were these men Normans or Saxons?

The motte has been embroidered with stripes in different colours. Is this meant to show that mottes were made of alternate layers of soil and stone, or was this done just to make the tapestry look more attractive?

How big was the motte? It is difficult to tell because nothing was in proportion in the Bayeux Tapestry.

What can research reveal about early Norman castles?

Castle-building after the Battle of Hastings

Following his success at the Battle of Hastings, William knew that it was vital to capture London. During the autumn of 1066, the Norman army marched through south-east England, devastating the territory around the capital. First, they headed east to Dover where they defeated a remaining Saxon garrison and built a third castle. William's army then marched through Kent and the Thames Valley. It is often difficult to be certain exactly when a castle was built, but historians think that the surviving mottes at Canterbury, Wallingford and Berkhamsted date from this time. When William finally entered London, he immediately began building a castle in the south-east corner of the city. (You can find out more about this castle in closer look 4 on pages 78 and 79.)

During the autumn of 1066, castles clearly played a vital role in the Norman invasion and conquest of England. The Normans started to build fortifications as soon as they arrived and used them to secure the south-east of the country. Some of these early castles were motte and baileys, but not all. Excavations at Pevensey, Dover and London have shown that these sites did not contain a motte. They were simply enclosures known as 'ringworks', built into the corner of existing fortifications. The Normans built whatever was easiest and most effective in order to conquer England.

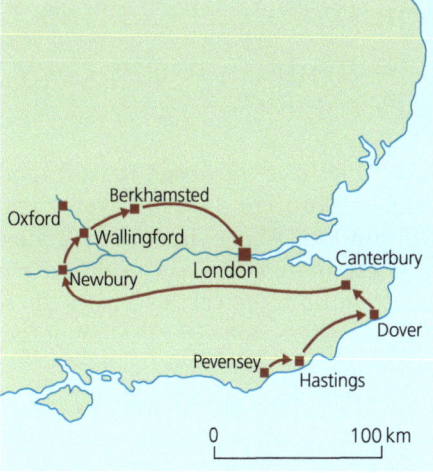

▲ A map of south-east England showing the castles which the Normans built in the autumn of 1066

Record

'The Normans introduced motte and bailey castles into England after 1066.'

1. List some points to show that this statement is correct.
2. List some points to show that the story of castles is more complicated than the statement suggests.
3. List some points to explain why it is difficult to be certain about Anglo-Saxon defences and the first Norman castles in England.

▼ A recent photograph of the motte and bailey castle at Berkhamsted. The stone defences were added later

Where were Norman castles built and what did they look like?

In March 1067, William returned to Normandy. The King left his half brother, Odo of Bayeux, and trusted friend, William FitzOsbern, in charge of his new kingdom. These men, based at Dover and Winchester, soon began to build more castles across the south of England. The *Anglo-Saxon Chronicle* recorded:

> Bishop Odo and Earl William were left behind here and they built castles far and wide throughout the land, oppressing the unhappy people, and things went from bad to worse.

The new Norman castles caused much suffering. The English were often forced to build castles by their new Norman lords. In towns, sometimes hundreds of houses were demolished to create space for a new castle. In some places, Norman soldiers may have ridden out from a castle, committing acts of plunder, rape and violence against local people. It is likely that castles soon became a detested symbol of Norman rule. As early as 1067, chroniclers recorded risings against the Norman castle-builders in several parts of England.

Castle building in the years of crisis, 1068–71

Towards the end of 1067, William received the news that a major rising was being planned in the south-west. He quickly returned to England. As you discovered in Enquiry 3, the next four years were a time of crisis for the Normans, with major rebellions in many parts of England.

The royal castles

William crushed the English revolts and established royal castles in many towns. Between 1068 and 1071, he built new royal fortresses at Exeter, Warwick, Nottingham and York.

Before the Norman Conquest, York was the most important city in the north of England. In 1068, William I built a motte and bailey castle there between the rivers Ouse and Foss. The huge motte was over 60 metres wide at its base. Following the 1069 rising in the north of England, William strengthened the castle and built another motte on the opposite bank of the River Ouse.

The King protected the road to the north by building royal castles at Lincoln, Cambridge and Huntingdon. These royal castles were the key to William's military conquest of England after 1067. Towering over the surrounding landscape, they also reminded the local population of the King's power and of his right to rule.

> ### Reflect
> 1. What details of the King's motte and bailey castle at York has Terry Ball included in his illustration?
> 2. How does Terry Ball's style as an illustrator compare with the style of Alan Sorrell (see the picture on page 66)?

▼ A painting of the motte and bailey castle at York, by the reconstruction artist Terry Ball

What can research reveal about early Norman castles?

Other castle-builders

William was not the only person to build castles in England. In the early years of the conquest, the king relied on a small number of trusted noblemen to establish Norman control in different parts of England:

- William divided Sussex into six new lordships and granted these to different barons who each built a castle. These castles were vital in protecting the routes from Normandy to London.
- The king granted vast territories to his half-brother, Robert of Mortain. In the west of England, Robert built several fortresses including a timber castle built on top of a steep hill at Montacute. Here Robert lived at the centre of his estates.
- William made his relative and trusted follower, William FitzOsbern, Earl of Hereford and granted him lands on England's dangerous border with Wales. Before 1071, FitzOsbern had built castles at Chepstow, Berkeley, Clifford and Wigmore.

The locations of these early castles built by William's barons were often carefully chosen to control rivers and roads. They were also often built on top of important Saxon sites as the Normans were determined to demonstrate their power and control.

What the castles looked like

The castles which the Normans built in the early years of the conquest were very different from the Saxon defences which existed in England before 1066. Norman castles were smaller, often taller and were occupied by a limited number of fighting men. It is difficult to be certain about the exact layout and design at each site, but it is clear that early Norman castles were not all alike:

- Most castles were probably timber motte and bailey structures like the one at York. However, the exact layout and construction of motte and bailey castles varied from place to place.
- Up to a quarter of the early castles may have been ringworks – simple enclosures of earth and timber, often built into the corner of an existing fortress like the ones at Pevensey and London.
- A small number of the early castles, like the King's castle in London and William FitzOsbern's castle at Chepstow, were built in stone.

▲ A map of the main Norman castles in England in 1071

◀ A recent photograph of Chepstow Castle. William FitzOsbern built the castle on top of the cliffs overlooking the River Wye. Chepstow guarded one of the main river crossings between England and Wales and was used as a base for conquering the Welsh kingdom of Gwent. Most of the ruins date from the thirteenth century, but parts of the early Norman stone castle remain

Castle building 1071–87

By 1071, five years after the Battle of Hastings, English resistance to the Norman Conquest had ended. The Normans had built around 35 castles across England and these had played an important role in enforcing Norman rule. In the years between 1071 and the death of William I in 1087, the Norman Conquest entered a new phase. Now the emphasis was on settling the land as well as keeping the country under control.

A huge increase in castle-building

It is impossible to say exactly how many Norman castles were built in the period 1071 to 1087, but the number was huge. *Domesday Book* – King William's great survey of England in 1086 – is a bit of let down when we try to work out how many castles the Normans built. It mentions only fifty castles, but we know from other written documents and from the evidence on the ground that there were many more castles than this. Historians have estimated that there were around 1,000 Norman castles in England and Wales by 1150. They think that around 500 of these may have been built during the reign of William the Conqueror. Whatever the exact number, there was a huge increase in castle-building after 1071:

1066–71 – around 35 castles
1071–87 – around 500 castles

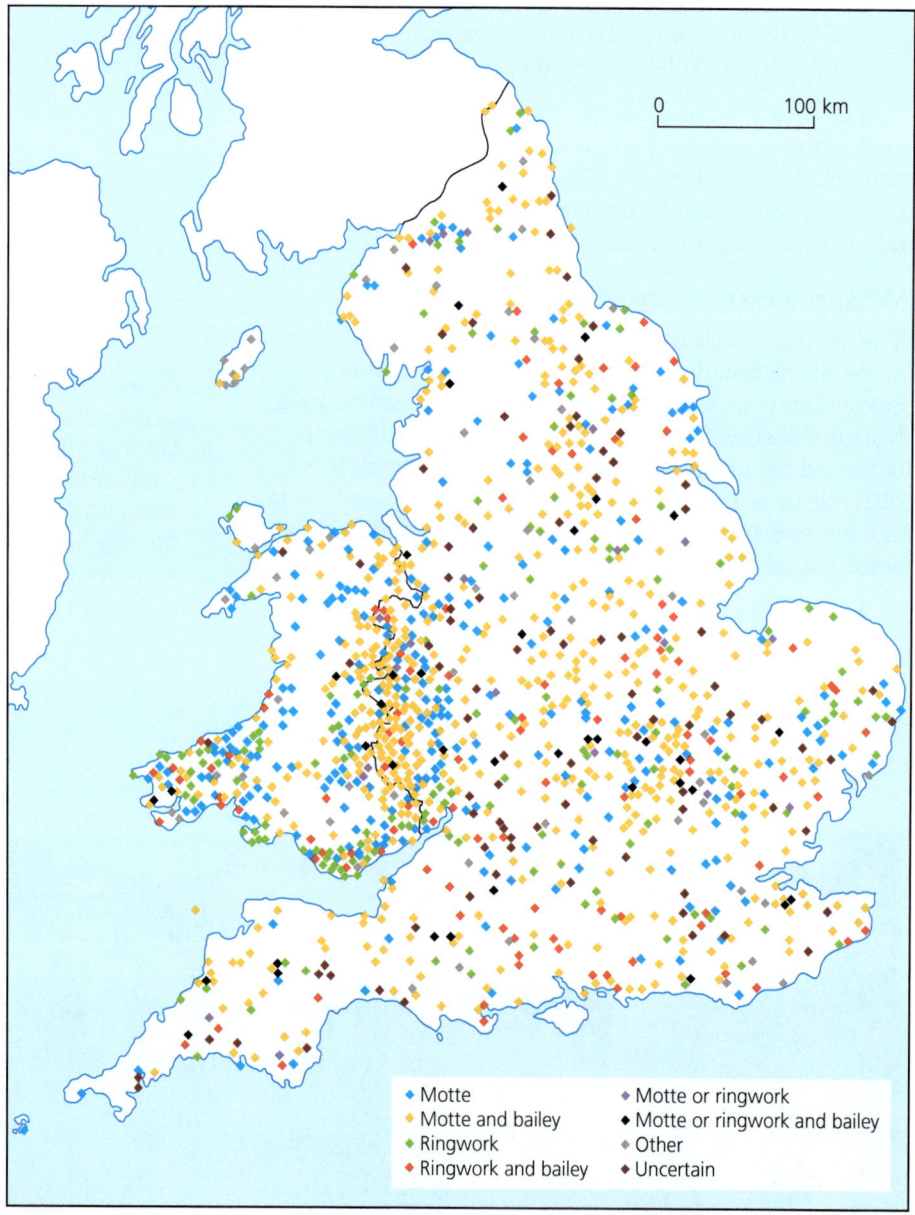

▶ A map showing the distribution of different types of Norman castles in England and Wales by 1150

Reflect

What can the map tell us about the:
1. distribution of early Norman castles
2. different types of castles which the Normans built?

What can research reveal about early Norman castles?

The castle builders

A number of castles built between 1071 and 1087 continued to be built on William's orders. For example, historians think that around the year 1080, the King ordered the building of motte and bailey castles on the sites of the Roman forts at Cardiff and Newcastle. However, most of the Norman castles built between 1071 and 1087 belonged not to the King, but to his barons and knights. After the defeat of the English rebellions, William distributed huge blocks of land to his barons, charging them with the task of maintaining control of their territories. The barons then granted land to their knights in return for military service. During the last sixteen years of William the Conqueror's reign, it was these Norman lords who built castles far and wide across the country.

The Norman castles built between 1071 and 1087 had more to do with settlement than with conquest. They were nearly all built in the countryside rather than in the towns. Some historians think that these castles did not really have an important military function. They argue that Norman lords used their castles to manage their lands and as symbols of power rather than as serious military fortresses. Other historians disagree and emphasise the military function of these minor castles.

What the castles looked like

Often, all that survives of the rural castles are overgrown earthworks. Sometimes, however, detailed research at one site can reveal what a minor castle looked like. In the 1970s, archaeologists investigated the timber motte and bailey castle at Goltho. Around the year 1080, a local Norman lord built his castle here on top of the fortified Saxon site (see page 64). The archaeological reconstruction below reveals what the early Norman castle at Goltho probably looked like.

▼ An archaeological reconstruction of the Norman castle at Goltho in Lincolnshire

Hall
Quite small. Unlikely that the Norman lord lived at Goltho. A steward probably lived here and looked after the manor for the lord

Ramparts
18 metres thick at the base and 4 metres high

Bailey
Quite small. The Saxon enclosure may have been used as an outer bailey for horses and storage

Gatehouse
The only entrance to the bailey

Bridge
18 metres long

Palisade
4 metres high

Moat
12 metres wide and 4 metres deep. Contained water

Tower
Guarded the entrance to the bailey and dominated the village. At least 9 metres high. Sloping sides made it stronger

Motte
23 metres wide and 5 metres high. Sides covered with alternate layers of stone and turf

Reflect

In your view, was the motte and bailey castle at Goltho a serious military fortress or did it mainly reflect the status and power of its owner?

Record

'In the years after 1066, William the Conqueror built a large number of motte and bailey castles to gain control of England.'

1. List some points to show that this statement is correct.
2. List some points to show that the story of castles is more complicated than the statement suggests.
3. List some points to explain why it is difficult to be certain about early Norman castles.

What exactly were early Norman castles for?

Historians have been studying early Norman castles for over a hundred years, but they still can't agree about what exactly castles were for. This is not because historians are useless or are unable to make up their minds. As you know, history changes because as new historians come along they ask new questions, make new discoveries and develop new ideas. Evidence can usually be interpreted in different ways so there is always room for discussion, debate and disagreement in history. This is exactly what has happened in the study of early Norman castles.

Record

The changing interpretations of castles are often based on new research. As you have discovered, written documents and pictures can only reveal a limited amount about early Norman castles. Research by archaeologists can reveal much more.

As you learn about four approaches used by archaeologists, list some points to explain what each approach has revealed about the purpose of early Norman castles.

Traditional interpretations

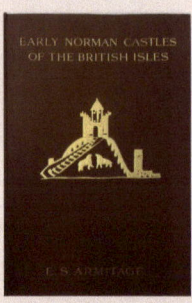

The front cover of Ella Armitage's 1912 book, *The Early Norman Castles of the British Isles*

At the beginning of the twentieth century, many people believed that the mottes which existed all over the country were built in the Roman and Saxon periods. Ella Armitage overturned this idea by using documents and maps to study hundreds of castles. In her 1912 book, she showed that it was definitely the Normans who first built mottes in England. Ella Armitage, and other historians working in the first half of the twentieth century, argued that castles played an important military role in the Norman Conquest. These historians lived at a time when warfare dominated the lives of people in Britain, so it is not surprising that they emphasised the military role of the castle.

Revisionist interpretations

The front cover of Robert Higham and Philip Barker's 1992 book, *Timber Castles*

In the 1960s, some people began to question the military interpretation of castles. When archaeologists began to research early Norman defences they discovered that many of the earliest Norman castles were ringworks. These structures were also built by the Anglo-Saxons and this led some archaeologists to suggest that Norman castle-building was not particularly new. Other revisionist historians began to examine the features of remaining stone castles and discovered that many were quite weak. They argued that castles must have been more about showing off the status of the owner than about serious defence. In their 1992 book, *Timber Castles*, Richard Higham and Philip Barker suggested that the wooden castles built by the Normans were also often designed to show the status of their owners.

Recent interpretations

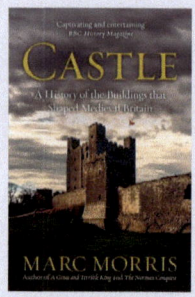

The front cover of Marc Morris's 2012 book, *Castle*

In recent years, some historians have argued that the revisionist interpretation has gone too far. In their view, early Norman castles were far more than expressions of status and power. Castles were military fortresses which played a crucial role in the brutal Norman occupation of England after 1066. They point out that early Norman castles were heavily-defended sites containing garrisons of Norman cavalry which could have inflicted great damage on the local English populations. In 2012, the historian Marc Morris wrote, 'castles have to be regarded first and foremost as military installations, introduced to subdue an unwilling population'.

What can research reveal about early Norman castles?

Approach 1: Examining stone structures

Because so few early Norman castles were built in stone, any surviving stone structures from the period 1066–87 are worth careful examination. At Exeter, a very rare stone gatehouse still survives. Most people who walk past it probably have no idea how special it is!

In 1068, after William defeated the English rebels at Exeter, he ordered his men to begin building a castle in the north-east corner of the city where the ground was highest. The Normans used part of the existing Roman walls which had been strengthened by King Athelstan in the tenth century. As you can see from the plan on the right, the Normans built a ditch and rampart to create a square enclosure. They also built a large stone gatehouse into the south side of the enclosure.

When archaeologists made a careful study of the Exeter castle gatehouse, they were surprised by some of its features:

- The gatehouse was built facing *into* the city.
- The blocked entrance was originally a large gateway with wooden doors.
- Above the entrance was a chamber with two large triangular-headed windows – an Anglo-Saxon design.

Some historians and archaeologist have argued that we should not think of the Exeter gatehouse as a defensive structure. Its design was very much like the wooden gatehouses of the Saxon thegns which were intended to show the status of their owners.

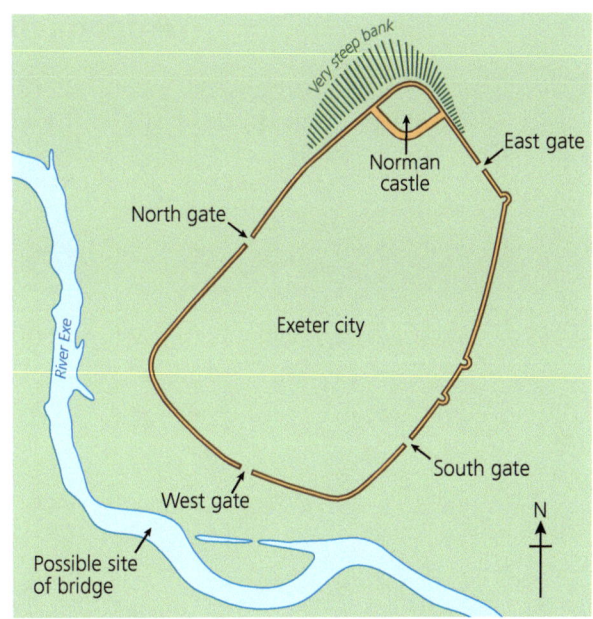

▲ Exeter in 1068

Reflect

In what ways does the evidence from Exeter castle suggest that early Norman castles were status symbols?

▲ A recent photograph of Exeter castle gatehouse

▲ A reconstruction drawing of the Exeter castle gatehouse

Approach 2: Surveying earthworks

▲ The earthworks at Elmley Castle, Worcestershire, from the air

> **Reflect**
>
> In what ways does the evidence from earthwork surveys suggest that early Norman castles were serious military fortresses?

Most early Norman castles were built not with stone, but with earth and timber. The timber palisades and towers decayed long ago, but often the earthwork defences survive. Historic England, the organisation which looks after these historic sites, estimates that around 700 earthwork castles still survive in England. Many of these date from the period before 1087.

Archaeologists can study earthworks by using aerial photographs or by making detailed surveys at the sites. Surveys have revealed two main types of earthworks, but within each type there was a huge variety of structures.

1. **Ringworks** were simple enclosures. They were often oval, but varied in shape. Soil from a ditch was used to make a large inner bank which would have been topped with a timber palisade. Sometimes the Normans built a full ring, but often they could build a partial ring by using natural features or existing fortifications.
2. **Mottes** were often built from soil thrown up from a surrounding ditch. However, at some sites they were formed from natural hills or from prehistoric burial mounds. Some mottes were steep and narrow, others were low and broad. They sometimes stood alone, but were often linked to one, or sometimes two, baileys.

The aerial photograph above shows the earthworks at Elmley Castle in Worcestershire. This is a complex site where a Norman ringwork was built on top of an Iron Age fort. The first castle dates from around 1080, but the earthworks survey also revealed the buildings of a later medieval castle.

What can research reveal about early Norman castles?

Approach 3: Looking at landscapes

In the 1980s, researchers began to take a wider look at castles. Instead of just focusing on the defended site, archaeologists started to investigate the wider landscapes surrounding castles. This research strengthened the revisionist interpretation that many castles had little to do with military conquest. Three important findings emerged from the landscape approach:

1. More than 80 per cent of castles were located in the countryside. Many of these rural sites were not well defended and it was hard to find any military explanation for their location. Most early Norman castles were situated at the centre of the lord's estate and were important centres for the administration of land.
2. Castles were often inserted into Saxon landscapes. They were sometimes built close to burh-geats (see page 64) which had belonged to Saxon thegns. Often there was a Saxon settlement or church nearby.
3. Norman lords soon began to change the landscape around their castle to make it look more impressive, as was done at Castle Acre in Norfolk.

Castle Acre

The aerial photograph below shows the landscape around Castle Acre. In 1066, there was already a settlement and church here belonging to an Anglo-Saxon thegn called Toki. Around 1070, the Norman lord William de Warenne built a castle here, at the centre of his Norfolk estates. This was a two-storeyed house built in the centre of a ringwork. In the early 1080s, William brought a small community of monks to Castle Acre who began to build a priory nearby. In the early twelfth century, the de Warenne family created a more impressive castle as a symbol of their wealth and power. They created a deer park and even diverted a Roman road to give more impressive views of their castle.

> ### Reflect
> In what ways does the evidence from Castle Acre support the interpretation that early Norman castles were status symbols?

▼ A recent aerial photograph of Castle Acre, Norfolk

The earthworks of the castle

The ruins of the priory

Approach 4: Digging castle sites

Archaeological digs can reveal a lot about early timber castles, but excavations are expensive and only a few sites have been investigated in this way.

One motte and bailey castle which has been studied in great detail over many years is Hen Domen. The castle was built by one of William the Conqueror's closest friends – Roger de Montgommeri. Soon after his victory in 1066, the King made Roger Earl of Shrewsbury and granted him vast estates on the English–Welsh border. In 1070, Hen Domen was one of the castles which Roger built to secure this dangerous territory.

Today, the earthworks at Hen Domen are overgrown with trees and bushes, and hardly anyone visits the site. But every summer from 1960 until 1992, Hen Domen was busy with archaeologists digging and carefully recording their discoveries. Thanks to the work done at Hen Domen we now know a lot more about the structure and purpose of early Norman castles.

Over the years, archaeologists uncovered many complex layers in the development and re-building of Hen Domen. Below is a summary of what they discovered about the first castle at the site.

> **Reflect**
>
> In what ways does the evidence from Hen Domen support the interpretation that early Norman castles were serious military fortresses?

▼ The excavation of Hen Domen. If you look closely you can see the archaeologists' tents

At the top of the motte, archaeologists uncovered the foundations of a large tower. This would have given a distant view of the surrounding roads and allowed Roger's men to control the crossing point on the River Severn.

The castle was defended by double ramparts and deep ditches. This would have made it very difficult to attack. Archaeologists thought that a tall timber palisade stood on top of the ramparts.

Archaeologists dug for over 30 years, but they still only managed to investigate half of the bailey. They found a large wooden building which was probably the great hall. The bailey also contained a granary (a building for storing grain), a cistern (a stone container for water) and several smaller buildings which were probably workshops.

Archaeologists were disappointed to discover few 'small finds' such as jewellery and coins. The most exciting find was half a bucket! The lack of luxury items revealed that Hen Domen was an important military site, manned by knights and soldiers who lived in tough conditions, not a castle built to reflect Roger's status.

What can research reveal about early Norman castles?

There is still lots to discover about early Norman castles, but research by historians and archaeologists has revealed a much more complex and interesting story of castle-building after 1066 than is often presented in books, heritage guides and websites.

Record

'Norman castles were brutal buildings built to suppress the Saxons.'

1. List some points to show that this statement is correct.
2. List some points to show that the story of castles is more complicated than the statement suggests.
3. List some points to explain why it is difficult to be certain about what exactly Norman castles were for.

Review

The information below about Norman castles is from the history learning website: www.historylearningsite.co.uk

Read the text carefully and identify the points which are incorrect and those which are too simplistic.

> The Normans were master castle builders. After 1066, England witnessed a massive castle-building programme on the orders of William the Conqueror. First, motte and bailey castles were built. Once William had firmly established his rule in England, he built huge stone-keep castles.
>
> Castles were a very good way for the Normans to expand their grip on the English people. The English population greatly outnumbered the Normans and the Normans had to create an atmosphere in which they were feared by the English, therefore, minimising the possibility of an uprising by the English.
>
> Castles were a sign of Norman power and might. They could be easily seen and so acted as a deterrent. The castles warned the English that Norman soldiers lived in these castles and that any attempts to rise up against them would be met with force.
>
> The castles also gave the Norman soldiers a safe place to live. They were, after all, invaders. William had built a temporary castle at Pevensey to house his troops when they landed in September 1066. This would have been a motte and bailey. These types of castles were quickly put up all over England after the Battle of Hastings to enforce Norman control.

Now design three new web pages which provide a more accurate, complex and interesting account of early Norman castles in England. Use the following headings for your pages:

- Page 1: The first Norman castles in England
- Page 2: The distribution and design of castles in England, 1067–87
- Page 3: Debates about the purpose of early Norman castles

CLOSER LOOK 4

The Tower of London

This is one of the most famous buildings in the world – the Tower of London. Historians think that the Normans began to build the Tower between 1075 and 1079, and that it was finished after William's death in 1087. This was the Conqueror's main fortress, royal palace and centre of govenment.

> **Reflect**
> Read the information below and look carefully at the photograph. In what ways did the Tower of London provide the King with a secure fortress.

The fake upper floor
Over the centuries, nearly all windows on the Tower have been enlarged, but three pairs of Norman windows remain on the upper floor. The windows gave the illusion of an upper floor. In fact, there was just a roof and a narrow walkway where Norman soldiers patrolled.

The second floor
This contained the King's apartments. Here, you can still visit the Chapel of St John, which looks much as it did in Norman times. The King's fireplaces and garderobe (latrine) also remain. A spiral staircase was the only access to the second floor.

The entrance floor
The entrance was above ground level. A wooden staircase could be removed if the castle was under attack. The entrance floor probably included the King's throne room. His officials would have used the floor when he was elsewhere.

The basement
This was used as a store. It included a well which ensured a supply of water.

▶ A recent photograph of the White Tower

What can research reveal about early Norman castles?

Building the Tower

Today, the Tower of London still stands on the north bank of the River Thames. It is one of the most visited historic sites in England. As you can see from this aerial photograph, the original Norman Tower has been extended and strengthened over the centuries. This makes it hard to imagine what the site was like at the time of the Norman Conquest. The reconstruction painting below, by the artist Ivan Lapper, brings the site to life.

We know that William began to build fortifications at this site shortly after he took control of London in the autumn of 1066. He chose the south-east corner of the Roman walls which still surrounded London at that time. The River Thames provided additional protection to the south. The Normans quickly built a ditch and earth bank with a wooden palisade. Ivan Lapper's painting shows the site when construction of the stone tower had just begun.

▲ A recent aerial photograph of the Tower of London

▼ A reconstruction painting of the building of William's first fortress at the Tower of London, by Ivan Lapper

Reflect

What interesting details has Ivan Lapper included in his painting?

5

'A truck-load of trouble'

What was the impact of the Norman Conquest on the English by 1087?

▶ A recent aerial photograph of Old Sarum

Three kilometres to the north of modern Salisbury lies one of the most important historic sites in England: Old Sarum. In 1070, William the Conqueror chose this huge Iron Age hill fort as the location for one of his royal castles. In the centre of Old Sarum, the King built a massive motte. The enormous bailey around the motte gave another layer of protection. After 1075, in the bailey of Old Sarum, the Normans began to build Salisbury's first cathedral.

Old Sarum became one of the great centres of power in Norman England. William thought it was a perfect place for the large, open-air gathering which he planned in the summer of 1086. Twenty years after his victory at Hastings, the King ordered all the powerful men in England to make their way to Old Sarum for a special ceremony.

In August 1086, archbishops, bishops, abbots, earls, barons and knights from all over England gathered at the King's great castle. Historians do not know exactly how many men met at Old Sarum, but it is likely to have been in the thousands. Nearly all of them were Norman. In the two decades since the invasion of 1066, the Anglo-Saxon nobles and churchmen had been stripped of their land, power and titles.

Two extraordinary rituals took place at Old Sarum on 1 August 1086. First, in an open-air ceremony, each of the Norman nobles knelt in front of their king and swore an oath of loyalty to him. Then, William was presented with seven thick, parchment documents. These contained the results of the greatest national survey ever seen in England. It would become known as *Domesday Book*.

What was the impact of the Norman Conquest on the English by 1087?

William knew that such a public display of loyalty and power would reinforce his position as the undisputed ruler of England. But he could not have known that just over a year later his reign in England would come to an end. Not long after the ceremony at Old Sarum, the Conqueror crossed the English Channel for the last time. William was in his late fifties and years of eating too much meat had made him very large. But the King's age and size did not stop him from taking part in military campaigns. In the summer of 1087, the Normans set fire to the French town of Mantes. During the attack, William's horse bucked and he was thrown violently against the hard pommel at the front of his saddle. The King began to bleed internally. He never recovered. On Thursday 9 September 1087, William the Conqueror died.

Reflect

How does Peter Dunn portray the drama and importance of the events at Old Sarum on 1 August 1086?

The Enquiry

For the people of Anglo-Saxon England, the events of 1066 to 1087 must have been a traumatic experience. In his book *A History of Britain*, the historian Simon Schama used a striking phrase to describe the impact of the Norman Conquest on the English: he called it 'a truck-load of trouble'. In this enquiry you will find out about the impact of the Norman Conquest on the English by 1087 and explain how it caused them so much trouble. You will begin by exploring the remarkable document which tells us so much about the transformation of England in the period 1066–87: *Domesday Book*.

▼ William the Conqueror receiving his barons at Old Sarum in August 1086. A painting by the reconstruction artist Peter Dunn

Domesday Book

William I spent Christmas 1085 at Gloucester. It was a worrying time. A Danish army had joined forces with the Count of Flanders and was threatening to invade England. This was one of the biggest crises of William's reign. The King held court for five days and then spent another three days on Church business. The *Anglo-Saxon Chronicle* tells us that he had 'great thought and deep conversation' with his council. He came up with an unexpected plan – he ordered a survey of the country he had conquered after 1066. This would provide a record of every piece of land and property in his kingdom. It would be a complete list of who owned what in England, down to the last pig.

The making of *Domesday*

The result of William's survey was a remarkable document: *Domesday Book*. Two things are immediately surprising about *Domesday Book*:

1. **It is not a single book.** Originally *Domesday* was two books: *Little Domesday* covered the counties of Essex, Norfolk and Suffolk; *Great Domesday* covered the rest of England, apart from the northern counties which were outside the control of the King. The photograph below shows *Domesday* as it exists today in The National Archives, London. In 1986, to conserve the documents, *Great Domesday* was rebound as two books and *Little Domesday* as three.

2. **Its official name was not *Domesday Book*.** In the eleventh and twelfth centuries *Domesday* was kept in the royal treasury at Winchester. Government officials called it the Book of Winchester, the Book of the Treasury or simply the King's Book. It was the English people who came up with a name that reflected its true power. They called it *Domesday* – the Day of Judgement. What was written in *Domesday Book* was final. There was no going back.

No other country in the world has such a detailed single record dating from so far back in time. *Domesday's* pages are crammed with information about England nearly a thousand years ago. The two million words in *Domesday Book* paint an incredible picture of the upheaval caused by the Norman Conquest.

▼ A photograph of *Domesday Book* in The National Archives after its new binding in 1986

What was the impact of the Norman Conquest on the English by 1087?

The survey

Collecting the information for *Domesday* was a massive task. William organised the thirty-four English shires into seven circuits (regions) and appointed four commissioners to collect the information in each circuit. William's commissioners focused on all the individual manors in their circuit. They asked the same questions about each of the 13,400 English manors.

The commissioners began with two basic questions:

- What is the name of the manor?
- How many hides are there? (A hide was a plot of land of around 120 acres.)

They asked about the resources of the manor:

- How many ploughs?
- How many mills?
- How many fisheries?

... and about the type of land:

- How much woodland?
- How much pasture?
- How much meadow?

They also asked about the people who lived on the manor:

- How many freemen?
- How many villeins?
- How many slaves?

Crucially, the commissioners collected information about each manor for two different dates: first, the day on which Edward the Confessor died in 1066; then, the day in 1086 when the survey took place.

Their last question was about the value of the manor:

- How much was it worth then?
- How much is it worth now?

All this information gave William vital knowledge about how the ownership and value of his kingdom had changed during the Conquest.

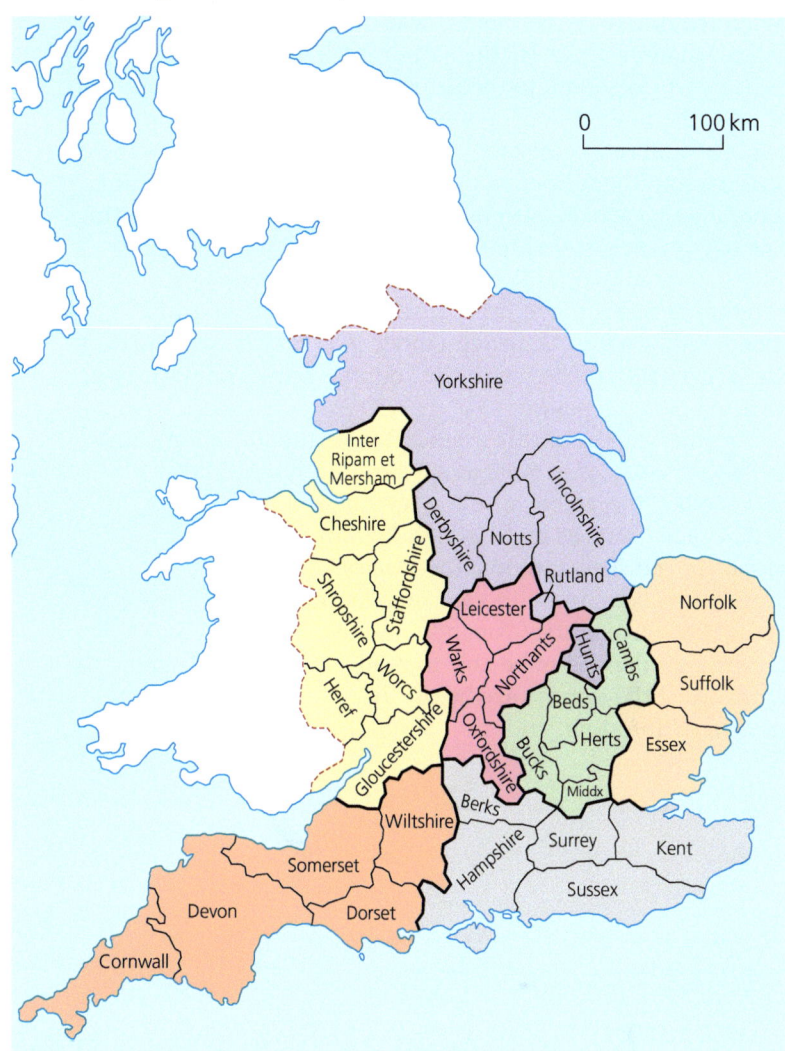

▼ A map showing the seven *Domesday* circuits

Reflect

Which counties are in the circuit where you live?

The inquests

Collecting all this information in just six months was a challenging task, particularly because there had been rapid and confusing changes in landownership during the twenty years of the Norman Conquest. Some people had written documents to prove that they owned a piece of land. Others had been granted land by William verbally and had no written proof. During the spring of 1086, in every county across England, jurors from each hundred (group of manors) travelled to special sessions of the shire court known as inquests. At the inquests, jurors listened to the evidence from witnesses and made life-changing decisions about who owned what. Everyone knew that the decision would be final. For many people, both Saxon and Norman, this must have been an incredibly stressful time.

The book

When the ordeal of the inquest was over, each group of commissioners wrote up their findings. These were the seven documents presented to the King at Old Sarum. In the autumn of 1086, the huge task of condensing all this information into a single final record began. It has often been said that a single scribe wrote *Great Domesday*, but some historians now think there may have been several scribes with similar handwriting. The document was written by hand using sharpened goose quills. Around two million words were written on 832 parchment pages made from the skins of 200 calves and sheep. William's death in September 1087 may be what ended the writing up process, with the counties still to be written-up forming *Little Domesday*.

As you can see in this extract for the manor of Patcham in Sussex, *Domesday Book* was written in Latin. The text is easy to read because the writing is so clear and because scribes highlighted the name of each manor in red. You can read the *Domesday* entries for the manors in your own areas using the website http://opendomesday.org. You don't need to be able to read Latin as all the entries are helpfully translated into English.

◀ A goose quill

▼ The entry in *Great Domesday* for Patcham in Sussex

What was the impact of the Norman Conquest on the English by 1087?

What was *Domesday Book* really for?

Domesday is a remarkable record, but nobody can be sure exactly why William commissioned his amazing survey. Over the years, historians have put forward different interpretations about the reasons for the *Domesday* survey.

For many years, historians believed that taxation was the reason for *Domesday Book*. They thought that William simply wanted to produce a massive tax database so that he could squeeze more money out of England. In 1086, William desperately needed more cash to defend England against the threatened Viking invasion. The theory seemed to be supported by William's instruction that his commissioners should note where 'more could be taken than is now being taken'.

More recent historians are less convinced that *Domesday Book* was a giant tax inventory. They have pointed out that it is not laid out in a way that would be helpful for anyone collecting taxes. As you can see on this example for Berkshire in *Domesday Book*, the opening page for each county lists the owners of land, giving a number which allows you to find their manors in the pages that follow. But this is useless for collecting tax. A tax collector would have needed the document to be set out geographically, village by village.

So, if *Domesday Book* was not intended to be a tax book, what was its real purpose? Many historians now believe that *Domesday Book* was an efficient way for the Normans to establish their legal right to own English lands. It confirmed the Norman lords as legitimate owners of the lands they had taken from the English. More importantly, *Domesday Book* demonstrated that William I was the undisputed ruler of England. It confirmed the Conqueror as the legal heir to King Edward and demonstrated that Norman nobles held their lands through the power and authority of the King. In this way, *Domesday Book* was a powerful instrument of royal power and control.

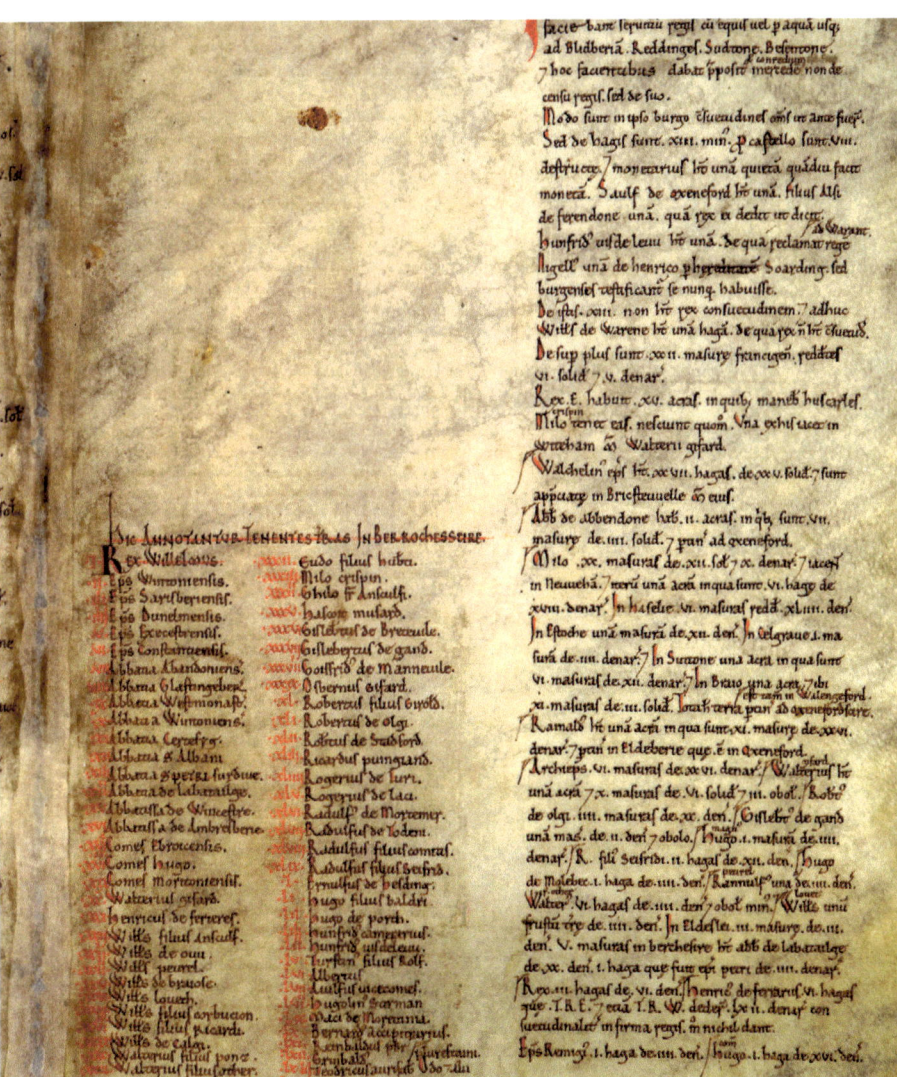

◀ The opening page for the county of Berkshire in *Domesday Book*

Record

Imagine that a historian is being interviewed about *Domesday Book* for a new documentary programme on the Norman Conquest. Work with a partner and write the script for the interview. Include five or six good questions which you think will help the audience to understand the interesting and important things about *Domesday Book*. Then write the clear and accurate answers given by the historian. When you have written your script, you could perform it, or record it, with your partner.

The impact of the Norman Conquest on the English people, 1066–87

In 1086, around two million people lived in England. Only around 20,000 – roughly one per cent of the population – were Norman. It is remarkable to think that twenty years after the invasion of 1066, this relatively small group of Normans owned nearly all the land in England. These Norman incomers had a profound impact on many aspects of life in England.

Record

Over the next eight pages you will find out about the impact of the Norman Conquest on the English people by 1087. As you learn about different aspects, make notes under the following headings:

1. Losing the land
2. Earning a living
3. Laws, language and the Church

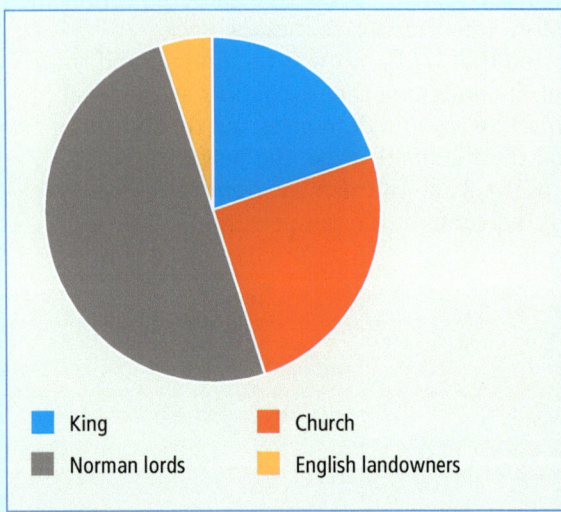

▲ The distribution of land in England in 1086

Losing the land

Following their success at the Battle of Hastings, William's men were hungry for reward. The Conqueror fed them with the lands of English earls and thegns who had died at Hastings. At first, William allowed the English nobles who had survived to keep their lands, but he changed this policy following the rebellions over the next four years. The Norman Conquest soon turned into a massive land-grab. As you can imagine, the effect on the English elite was devastating.

New lords

Domesday Book reveals that hardly any English thegns had held on to their land by 1086. Of the 180 tenants-in-chief who owned the largest estates, only four were English. Among the smaller sub-tenants we find more English landholders, but many of these men were leasing land from Norman lords which they had held freely in 1066. Historians estimate that by the time of *Domesday* the King held around 20 per cent of the land in England, with the Church holding another 25 per cent. The Norman secular lords held around 50 per cent, leaving just 5 per cent still in the hands of English landowners. As a result of the Norman Conquest, nearly all English landowners had been dispossessed of their land.

During the years 1066–87 many of the English elite migrated to Scotland, Ireland, Scandinavia and other parts of Europe. For those who remained, the sadness of individuals is sometimes revealed on the pages of *Domesday*. The English landholder Aelfric of Marsh Gibbon in Buckinghamshire, who owned his land freely in King Edward's time, now held it from the Norman Lord Ansculf 'at rent, heavily and miserably'. For many English landowners like Aelfric, the Norman Conquest had ruined their lives.

What was the impact of the Norman Conquest on the English by 1087?

Alan Rufus – a case-study of a new Norman lord

Alan Rufus, Count of Brittany and a second cousin to William the Conqueror, played a leading role at the Battle of Hastings. In the months after the battle, Alan's forces headed north to Cambridge where they began to build a castle. William gave Alan land in Cambridgeshire which was owned by King Harold's mistress, Edith the Fair.

In 1069, Alan helped to put down the rebellion in the north and the King rewarded him with the Honour of Richmond and other lands in Yorkshire. Much of this territory had previously been held by Edwin, Earl of Mercia. This picture, from a fifteenth-century book, shows William granting the Honour of Richmond to Alan Rufus.

By 1086, *Domesday Book* records that Alan owned lands in twelve different shires across England. These gave him an income of £1,100 a year, which would make him a billionaire today. Alan was the sixth richest Norman in England, but his lands were scattered and were not as large as the vast territories which had belonged to the Anglo-Saxon earls. King William ensured that none of his nobles was in a position to challenge his power.

New lordship

New Norman lords like Alan Rufus ruled their lands in a very different way from the English elite:

- Anglo-Saxon thegns usually had only one name, but the Normans often attached a place name to their first name to show they owned a particular piece of land.
- Anglo-Saxon thegns had divided up their property when they died, but the Normans made sure it passed entirely to the eldest son.
- The Normans built castles at the centres of their estates and often ruled their lands harshly.

These changes had serious consequences, not only for those at the top of Saxon society, but for all English people.

▲ William the Conqueror granting the Honour of Richmond to Alan Rufus in 1071. From a fifteenth-century illuminated manuscript

Reflect
What had made Alan Rufus such an important landowner in England by 1086?

Record
Start your notes on 'Losing the land'.

Earning a living

▲ A picture of peasants ploughing in an eleventh-century manuscript

The Norman Conquest had severe consequences for ordinary people in England. In some parts of the country, the first few years of the Norman Conquest caused widespread death and destruction. The 'Harrying of the North' led to so much devastation that it took the region many years to recover. *Domesday Book* shows that in 1086 the population of Yorkshire had dropped to just a quarter of what it had been in 1066. In areas of the country which did not experience rebellion, the impact of the Normans was not as devastating, but few English families were unaffected by the Norman Conquest.

Life on the manor

After 1066, England continued to be a rural society with 90 per cent of the population working in agriculture. In many ways, the farming year continued as before the Conquest. At the end of winter, the plough teams still turned the soil in the village fields. In summer, the villagers still grew their vegetables and harvested their corn. Each day, English women still milked the cows and children still carried water from the well.

Despite these continuities in village life, the Norman Conquest brought big changes to the lives of English peasants. The number of Saxons who were free ceorls, fell dramatically. In the village of Bourn in Cambridgeshire, nine hides of land had been farmed by twenty free peasants in 1066. By 1086, more than half had become dependent peasants who were forced to pay rent to a lord for land which they had once owned. This pattern was repeated across England.

The Norman Conquest limited many people's freedoms and their ability to make a living. However, some historians think that the lives of those at the very bottom of the English society – slaves – improved as a result of the Norman Conquest. In 1066, slavery was already a thing of the past in Normandy. *Domesday Book* shows us that by 1086 the number of slaves in England had fallen by around twenty-five per cent.

Overall, the Norman Conquest made the majority of English families much poorer. This was because Norman lords squeezed as much wealth from their lands as they possibly could. On average, Norman landowners increased the income from their lands by thirty per cent between 1066 and 1086. Alan Rufus managed to push up the income from his Norfolk estates by forty per cent. The increased rents which Norman lords imposed on their manors must have forced many English families into desperate poverty.

At the same time, many lords introduced new restrictions which made the lives of the English peasants much more difficult:

- They often forced Saxons to build castles as part of the services which the peasants owed on the manor.
- In some places, the English were prevented from fishing in the lord's river and were no longer allowed to collect firewood in the lord's forest.
- Norman lords often charged peasants high fees for using their water mills to grind corn.
- There is no doubt that, for many English people, life on the manor became much harsher in the twenty years after 1066.

Reflect

What changes and continuities were there in rural life between 1065 and 1086?

What was the impact of the Norman Conquest on the English by 1087?

Towns, markets and taxes

This map shows English towns in 1086.

> **Reflect**
>
> Think of three good historical questions about the impact of the Norman Conquest on towns.

In 1086, ten per cent of English people earned their living in a town. Many of the burhs which had been created in late Anglo-Saxon England continued into the Norman period. In parts of southern England some existing Saxon towns expanded and a small number of new towns had been created by 1086. This is probably explained by the increase in trade between England and Normandy after the Conquest.

Overall, however, the Norman Conquest had a negative impact on English towns. In the early years of the Conquest, towns in rebellious areas were attacked and burned as the Normans fought to establish control. Castle-building in towns often resulted in the clearance of large numbers of houses and workshops. Some large towns such as York, Lincoln, Norwich and Oxford suffered a big fall in population. Many smaller towns were also badly affected. For example, *Domesday Book* tells us that Stafford had only 179 houses in 1086 and forty per cent of these were empty.

The markets held in many towns were an important way for English people to earn a living, but the Normans saw them as a valuable source of income. After 1066, Normans lords seized control of nearly all market-trading in England. In Cornwall, the Count of Mortain moved the market from one of his manors into his castle, forcing traders to pay higher rents and tolls. Across England, Norman control of local markets added to the burdens of English peasants.

The Norman Conquest also brought big increases in taxation. As you discovered in Enquiry 1, Anglo-Saxon England had an efficient system for the collection of tax in England – the geld. William made use of the geld to pay for the troops and mercenaries who brought England under control. In 1067 and 1068, he introduced huge increases in the geld. This pressure of increased taxation was maintained through the period to 1086. It was another factor which contributed to the misery of the English people in the aftermath of the Norman Conquest.

▲ Map showing English towns in 1086

▼ Norman coins

> **Reflect**
>
> How big was your nearest town in 1086?

> **Record**
>
> Make notes under the heading 'Earning a living'.

89

Laws, language and the Church

This is the opening page from one of the most important manuscript books in English history – the *Textus Roffensis*. It is known in English as 'The Book of Rochester'. Over the centuries, the *Textus Roffensis* has been lost and recovered several times. Around the year 1710, the book fell into a river when the boat carrying it overturned. You can still see the dark water stain on the page.

The *Textus Roffensis* was written by a monk at Rochester in Kent during the 1120s. The first part of the book includes nearly forty English laws stretching across five hundred years between 600 and 1100. These include a long list of fines for violent crimes in Anglo-Saxon England. For example, people had to pay 50 shillings for gouging out someone's eye and six shillings for stabbing a man in his genitals.

New laws

Included in the *Textus Roffensis* is an account of the Saxon trial by ordeal in which an accused person held a red-hot iron or plunged their hand into boiling water. If the wound healed, it was taken as a sign from God that the person was innocent. The *Textus Roffensis* gives details of an addition to these Saxon laws which William I introduced in England after 1066: trial by combat. When an Englishman was accused of a crime, and there were no witnesses, he was allowed to defend himself in a sword-fight with his Norman accuser.

Trial by combat is a good example of the way in which William the Conqueror preserved and adapted Anglo-Saxon laws. But the Normans also introduced two totally new laws which were particularly hated by the English:

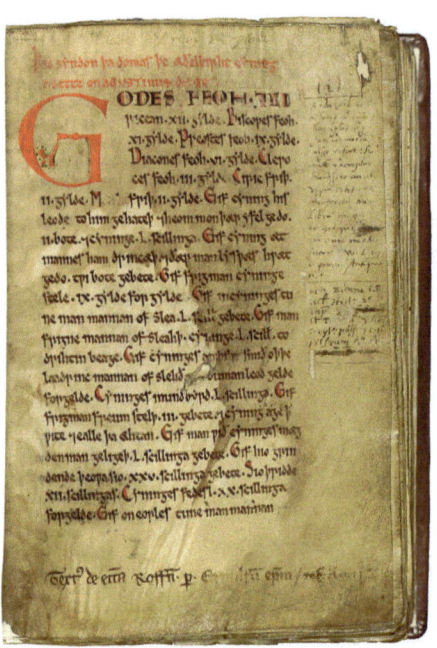

▲ The opening page of the *Textus Roffensis*

> **Reflect**
>
> Why do you think the new Norman laws were so hated by the English?

1. **The Murdrum Fine.** In the years after 1066, the Normans not only faced major rebellions, but also ambush and attack as they travelled along England's roads. William introduced a new law called 'murdrum' to deal with this. If any Norman was murdered, the local English community were forced to pay a crippling fine until the murderer was handed over for trial.

2. **Forest Law.** William I enjoyed hunting deer and wild boar. To preserve these animals, the King created royal forests. Forest law prevented the English from hunting in the royal forests and meant that they faced harsh penalties if caught. For hunting a small animal such as a rabbit, two fingers were chopped off. An Englishman who killed a deer in the royal forest would have his eyes gouged out.

What was the impact of the Norman Conquest on the English by 1087?

New language

The second part of *Textus Roffensis* is a collection of manuscripts relating to the history of Rochester Cathedral. The large and beautiful letter 'R', which you can see in the extract opposite, marks the beginning of this second section of the manuscript. Medieval scribes sometimes liked to show off their skill by turning important letters into pictures. Here, the scribe created the letter 'R' with a picture of Christ giving his blessing to the cathedral. At the same time, Christ is trampling on a beast which is meant to represent the devil.

> ### Reflect
> 1. Why do you think the scribe might have created this picture to start the second part of *Textus Roffensis*?
> 2. Look carefully at the text. What language do you think the scribe used when writing *Textus Roffensis*?

Like most of the manuscript books produced after the Norman Conquest, the *Textus Roffensis* was mainly written in Latin. This was a big change because before 1066 monks had mostly used English when writing manuscripts. The Norman Conquest brought a sudden end to the use of English as a written language. By 1070, most of the men in power could not understand English so the King's writing office stopped using it. Latin became the written language of government and of the Church.

Spoken language

More important for the English people was the change which the Norman Conquest brought to the spoken language. Before 1066, everyone in England, from the king to the poorest peasant, spoke English. After the Conquest, England's new rulers spoke Norman French while everyone else continued to use English. This reinforced the difference between the conquerors and the conquered. The use of two languages was a reminder to the English that they were now inferior people in their own country.

In the years following the Conquest, French and English began to blend together. French words were added to English, making it a richer and more varied language. At first these were the words of politics and law (*government, authority, justice, court*), but soon the language reflected Norman influence in other aspects of life (*music, melody, dance, love*). The differences between English and French were most obvious in relation to food. When an animal was in a mucky field it was English (*pig, sheep*), but when it was on a table with a glass of wine it was French (*pork, mutton*).

▲ A detail from *Textus Roffensis*

We now know that in the thousand years after the Norman Conquest, English would evolve to become one of the most widely-spoken and influential languages in the world. By the end of the Middle Ages, French was a foreign language which the educated English learned at school. But the English people who suffered the humiliation of the Norman Conquest could not have known this. For them, language was a symbol of their inferiority after 1066.

> ### Record
> Start your notes under the heading 'Laws, language and the Church' with points about laws and language.

Changes in the Church

In April 1070, William returned to the south of England following his 'Harrying of the North'. For Easter, he went to Winchester where he was joined by three representatives of the Pope. At the Winchester Easter court, the papal legates ceremonially crowned William. It was a transformative moment. In 1070, the Norman Conquest of England had been given the official approval of the Pope.

In the days following the crowning, the papal legates and the King had a series of meetings to reform and reorganise the English Church. They began at the top. Stigand was deposed as Archbishop of Canterbury and Lanfranc was appointed in his place. Thomas of Bayeux was chosen as the new Archbishop of York. New appointments of Norman bishops and abbots quickly followed. By 1080, only one of the sixteen English bishops remained in office and Norman abbots were in charge of nearly all English monasteries.

Rebuilding the cathedrals

As well as transforming the leadership of the English Church, the Norman Conquest led to an almost total rebuilding of England's cathedrals. The new Norman structures were generally much larger and more beautiful than the Saxon buildings they replaced. After 1070, work began on rebuilding the cathedrals at Canterbury, York, Winchester and Ely. Today, Durham Cathedral is the most complete example of a cathedral built in early Norman England. The great pillars which line the nave, and which you can see on this page, are a reminder of the powerful visual impact of the Norman Conquest.

Monasteries

In 1066, there were around 60 monasteries in England. In the north, many monasteries had been wiped out by the Viking invasions. The Norman Conquest led to a revival of monasticism. After 1070, new northern monasteries were built, or old ones restored, at Selby, Jarrow, Whitby, Durham and York. In many parts of England, the new Norman lords began to give gifts of land to abbeys 'back home' and looked to these abbeys to provide monks for the new English monasteries. The Norman Conquest resulted in a huge transfer of wealth from English monastic land to the great abbeys of Normandy and France.

▶ The nave of Durham Cathedral

What was the impact of the Norman Conquest on the English by 1087?

Parish churches

◀ St Mary's Church, Stoke-sub-Hamdon, Somerset

This is St Mary's Church at Stoke-sub-Hamdon in Somerset. Like many English parish churches it is a mixture of building from different periods. But St Mary's is special because the church contains so many fine Norman stone carvings. In the years after the Conquest, the Norman Lord Robert FitzIvo was granted the manor here. Robert built a fortified manor house next to the church. He spent a lot of money rebuilding St Mary's and making it look beautiful.

In the eleventh century, St Mary's would have looked very different from today. Although it was smaller (the tower was not built until the thirteenth century), the church looked very bright and colourful. Its lime-washed walls gleamed white in the sunshine. The carvings on the outside were all painted bright colours. Inside, the walls were covered in paintings and designs.

At the time of the Norman Conquest, England contained hundreds of parish churches. Only occasionally do traces of these Saxon churches survive (see page 22). The Normans destroyed them and built new churches in their place. They dedicated these new churches to their own saints. Only a handful of the Anglo-Saxon saints – St Botolph, St Eadburh, St Pega – survived. The new parish churches and saints transformed religion in England's villages and towns. They were another visual reminder to the English that their country was under foreign occupation.

▲ A stone carving from St Mary's Church, Stoke-sub-Hamdon, showing St George killing a dragon

Record
Finish your notes under the heading 'Law, language and the Church' with points about the Church.

Review
Use the notes from your work on pages 86–93 to write an essay explaining how far you agree with Simon Schama that the Norman Conquest brought a 'truck load of trouble' for the English.

CLOSER LOOK 5

The Norman Yoke

▲ In this image from the Luttrell Psalter, *c*.1330, the two pairs of oxen are each bound together by a yoke.

This picture from the fourteenth century shows peasants ploughing the fields with oxen, as they had done for centuries. Fastened around the necks of the oxen are wooden yokes which kept them under control. For some people, the yoke is a symbol of what the Normans did to the English people after 1066.

The Norman Yoke is based on two ideas:

1. Late Anglo-Saxon England was a 'golden age' when the English were a free and equal people who lived in a prosperous and well-ruled country. They had a flourishing culture and were united through language.
2. Following the Conquest, the English people lost their freedoms. They were robbed of their land and forced into poverty. The brutal and oppressive rule of the Normans imposed a foreign and unwanted culture on the English.

Your study of the Norman Conquest has shown that events of 1065 to 1087 were more complex than the black and white picture presented by the Norman Yoke. The Norman Yoke is a myth, but some historians think that it contains elements of truth. The Norman Yoke has certainly been very persistent over the last 950 years. This closer look examines how the myth of the Norman Yoke developed. In particular, it focuses on how the Norman Yoke has been reinforced through art and popular culture.

How the myth of the Norman Yoke developed

Orderic Vitalis was the first chronicler to use the word 'yoke'. In the early twelfth century, he wrote:

> The English lamented the loss of their freedoms and sought daily to shake off the yoke that was so burdensome.

Two hundred years after the Conquest, medieval chroniclers were still writing about the oppressive rule of the Normans.

During the English Civil War, in the seventeenth century, radical thinkers who were opposed to the king, argued that 600 years after the Conquest the English people were still being oppressed by the Norman Yoke. They looked back to the Saxon kings for a better model of kingship. One radical, John Hare, argued that because the aristocracy and gentry were descended from the Norman invaders, they should have their lands taken away from them. He even suggested that all French words should be removed from the English language.

Over the last three hundred years, the idea of the Norman Yoke has been reinforced through the writing of historians, politicians and novelists. The work of artists, children's writers and film-makers has also help to embed the myth in people's imagination. Let's have a closer look at three interesting examples …

The Norman Yoke

An 1844 painting

In 1844, there was a national competition to select works of art for the newly-built Houses of Parliament. It was decided that the rooms and corridors should be decorated with paintings of historical scenes relating to England's past. The artist Ford Madox Brown entered the painting below for the competition. He called it 'The Body of Harold'.

Brown's painting shows an imagined scene when the dead King Harold was brought before William after the Battle of Hastings. His choice of subject was deliberate. This was the evening when the freedoms which the English people had enjoyed under Saxon rule were crushed by the Norman Yoke.

The way in which Brown painted the scene shows that his loyalty was with the dead Saxon king. William the Conqueror sits on his horse at the top of the painting, but he and his officers are in the shadows. It is King Harold who dominates the picture. The dead king's large and powerful body still seems to have great force. Harold's face is unblemished in the evening sunshine. He still wears his crown and holds his battleaxe. Brown painted the dead Harold as a Saxon hero.

Brown was concerned about the inequality which was created by England's class system in the middle of the nineteenth century. In particular, he was critical of the inherited wealth and power of the aristocracy. His liberal politics made him sympathetic to the idea of Saxon freedoms crushed by a foreign nobility which still continued to control England 800 years later. Perhaps this is why his painting was not selected in the competition.

▲ The artist Ford Madox Brown c.1864

▼ 'The Body of Harold'. A painting by Ford Madox Brown, 1844

CLOSER LOOK 5

A 1961 comic strip

In 1950, Marcus Morris, a vicar from Southport, started a weekly children's comic called *Eagle*. The comic featured the science fiction story 'Dan Dare, Pilot of the Future', as well as other adventure stories, news and sport. *Eagle's* gripping content and high-quality illustrations made it immediately popular with British children (and some adults!). It was soon selling nearly a million copies a week.

In 1961, *Eagle* began to publish a comic strip version of the Norman Conquest on its centre spread. It was called 'Last of the Saxon Kings'. The series portrayed the Norman Conquest as a tragic story of the defeat of heroic King Harold by the nasty Duke William. Through the pages of *Eagle*, millions of children were introduced to the myth of the Norman Yoke.

The extract below portrays Harold and his men before and during the Battle of Hastings. It begins with Harold and his exhausted army on the evening before the battle. In the middle section, Harold is encouraging his men on the morning of the battle. In the bottom section, the action moves to the height of the battle and shows 'Harold and his gallant men' standing firm against the Norman attack'.

▶ 'Last of the Saxon Kings'. A comic strip in *Eagle*, 1961

The Norman Yoke

A 2014 film

This is a poster for the 2014 film, *The Hobbit: An Unexpected Journey*. The film was the first in a series of three fantasy adventure films directed by Peter Jackson. The films take place in the fictional world of Middle Earth. They follow the home-loving hobbit Bilbo Baggins who is persuaded by the wizard Gandalf the Grey to lead a quest to reclaim the Lonely Mountain from the dragon Smaug.

The 2014 film was based on a children's fantasy novel by J.R.R. Tolkien, published in 1937. Tolkien was a writer, poet and professor of Anglo-Saxon at Oxford University. Tolkien's novel came from his rich imagination, but he also drew on his knowledge of Anglo-Saxon culture and literature to create the world of Middle Earth. The Shire was the region of Middle Earth where the hobbits lived. On Tolkien's maps, the central part of the Shire corresponds to the Saxon kingdom of Mercia. This was the part of England where Tolkien had grown up as a boy. In the novels, the Shire is a peaceful and idyllic land where hobbits live in freedom, protected by the thain – their elected military leader. *The Hobbit* reinforces the myth of Anglo-Saxon England as a lost rural idyll.

Make up your own mind

Some historians are quick to point out that the romantic image of a Saxon 'golden age' is a long way from reality. They emphasise the brutality, inequality and slavery which existed in Saxon England. Others disagree and find much to admire in the government and culture of the Saxons. As you have discovered, historians also have different views about the transformation of England after 1066. For some, the Normans brought strong government and a rich culture to England. For others, the Norman Conquest was a destructive and brutal occupation which oppressed the English people. Hopefully, you now know enough about the Norman Conquest to make up your own mind.

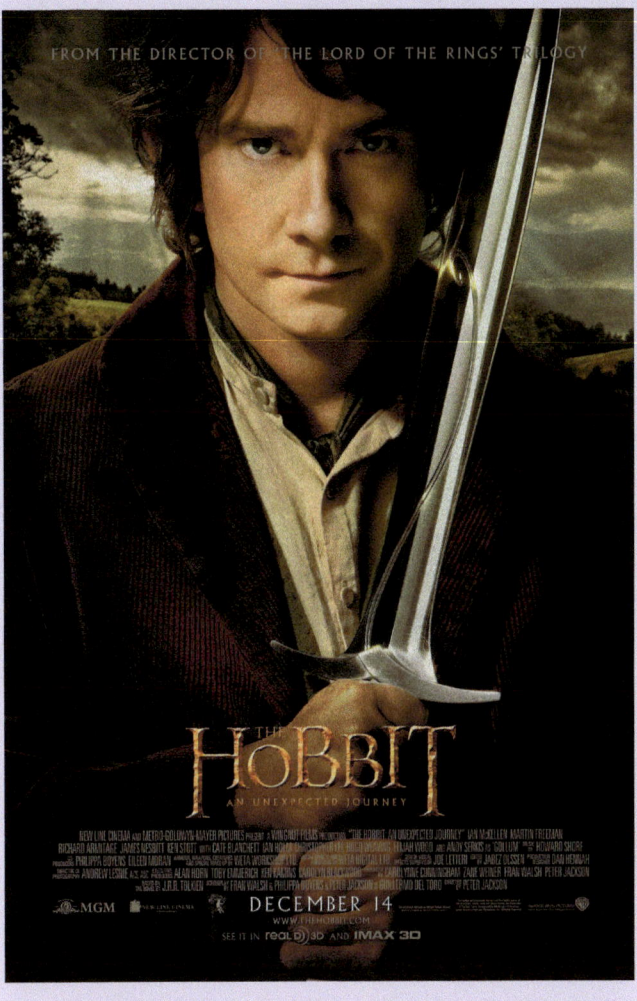

▲ A poster advertising the 2014 film, *The Hobbit: An Unexpected Journey*

◀ J.R.R. Tolkien's novel *The Hobbit*, first published in 1937

Preparing for the examination

The British depth study forms the second half of Paper 1: British History. It is worth twenty per cent of your GCSE. To succeed in the examination you will need to think clearly about different aspects of The Norman Conquest, 1065–1087 and support your ideas with accurate knowledge. This section suggests some revision strategies you might like to try and explains the types of examination questions that you can expect.

Summaries of the five key issues

Your study of The Norman Conquest, 1065–87, has covered five important issues from that time:

1. England on the eve of the conquest – the character of late Anglo-Saxon England c.1065
2. Invasion and victory – how and why William of Normandy became King of England in 1066
3. Resistance and response – the establishment of Norman rule between 1067 and 1071
4. Castles – the nature and purpose of Norman castles in England to 1087
5. Conquest and control – the impact of the Norman Conquest on English society to 1087

In the specification for your GCSE course, each of the five issues is divided into three sections.

We divided each enquiry in this book into three stages to match these sections and to help you build your knowledge and understanding step by step.

Now you can use your knowledge and understanding to produce a detailed and accurate summary for each of the five issues. You will also need to be clear about how the five issues are connected. Here are four suggestions for structuring your revision notes and showing the connections between the issues. Choose the one that is best for you or use a variety if you prefer.

1. Mind maps

A mind map on A3 paper (or even larger) is a good way to summarise the important points about a particular issue. It allows you to show connections between different points.

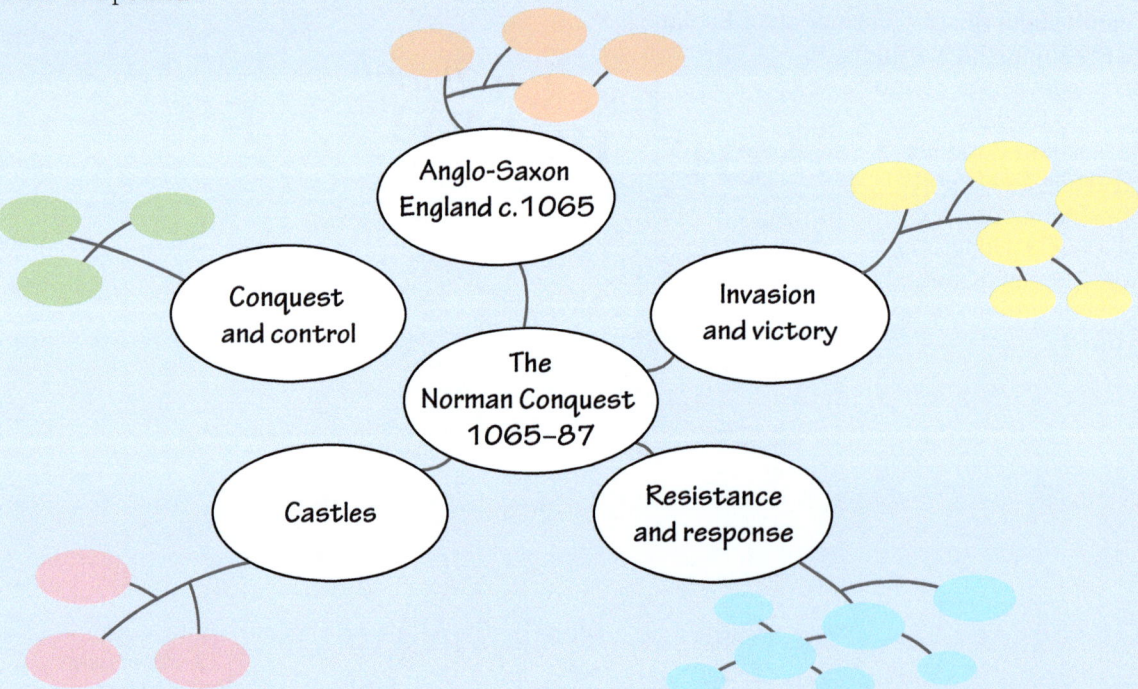

Preparing for the examination

2. Charts

If you find it easier to learn from lists then a summary chart for each issue you have studied might be best for you. You can use the format shown below or design your own. Just make sure that you include clear summary points for each of the three sections in each enquiry you studied.

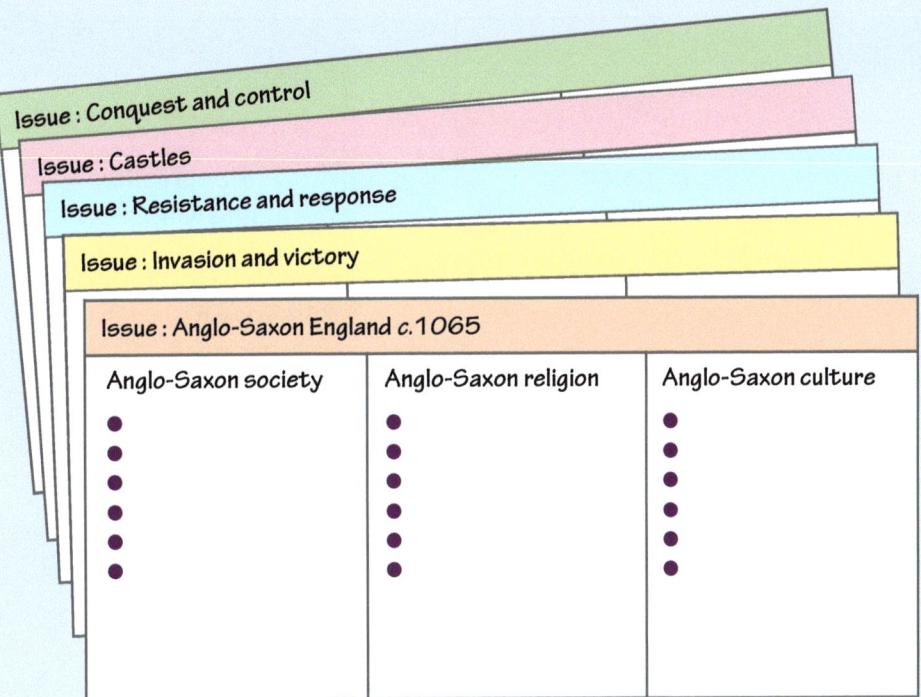

3. Small cards

Small cards are a flexible way to make revision notes. You could create a set of revision cards for each of the five main issues/enquiries you have studied. It would be a good idea to use a different colour for each set of cards.

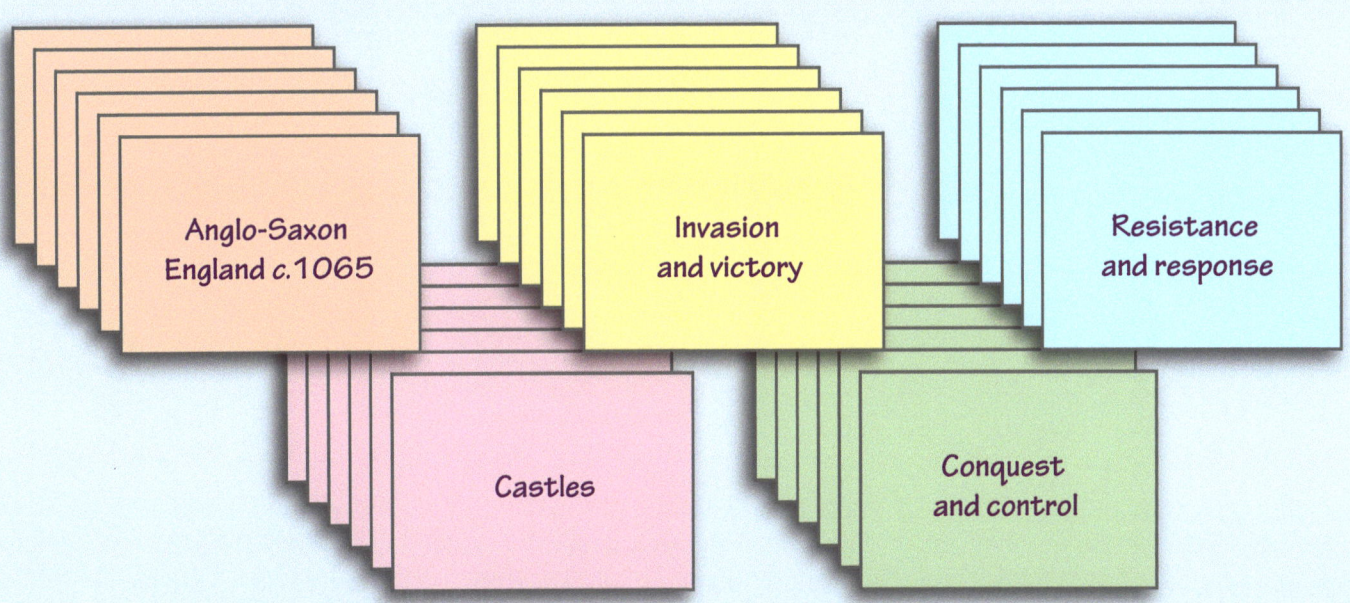

99

4. Podcasts

If you learn best by listening to information and explanations, you could record your knowledge and understanding by producing podcasts to summarise what you have learned about each of the five main issues. You could produce your podcast with a friend using a question and answer format.

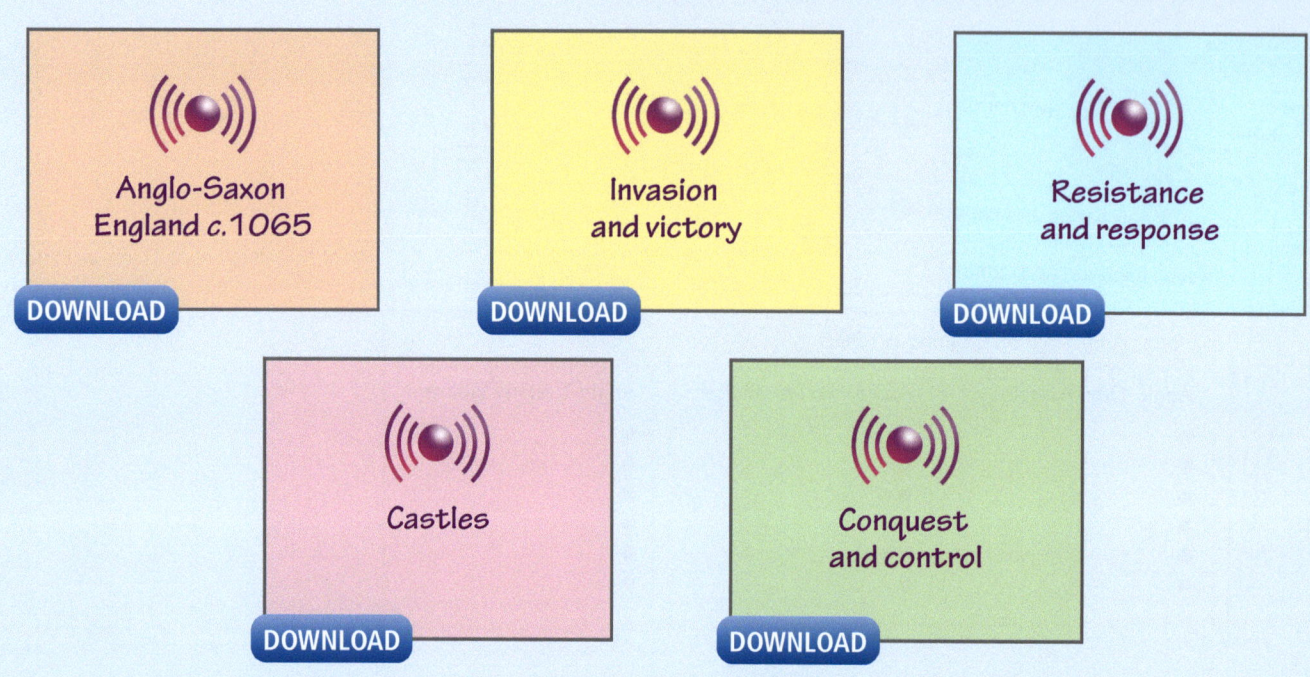

To be well-prepared for the examination you need revision notes that summarise the main points and provide detailed examples in a format that works best for you.

Preparing for the examination

 Understanding interpretations

To prepare for the examination, you will need to be clear about 'interpretations' of history. Here are some simple explanations and some suggestions for your revision.

What we mean by 'interpretations' of history

An interpretation of history is any version of events in the past that has been created at some later time. The interpretation can be made and shared by all sorts of people, in all sorts of ways, for all sorts of reasons. Here are some examples:

People or groups who create or advise on interpretations of the past	Ways in which interpretations may be shared	Reasons for creating interpretations of the past
Academics (professional historians, museum curators or archaeologists)	Non-fiction books	To educate or inform
	Fiction books	To entertain or amuse
	Websites	To persuade
Lecturers and teachers	Blogs	To commemorate
Writers and artists	Exhibitions and displays	
	Magazines	
Tourist organisations	Formal reports and articles	
	Plays	
Individuals or groups who are tracing the history of a family or an organisation	Films	
	Tourist information resources	
	Television/radio documentaries	
	Television dramas	
	Television light entertainment	
	Advertisements	
	Background to news reports	
	Drawings and paintings	
	Computer games	
	Theme parks	
	Souvenirs	
	Monuments	
	Ceremonies	

> **These tasks will help to sharpen your thinking about historical interpretations:**
>
> 1. Try to match up each of the people or groups in the left-hand column with the methods you think they might use to share their interpretations and the reasons why they have created them.
> 2. Look back through this book to find examples of historical interpretations. For each one that you find:
>   - briefly summarise what historical point it makes
>   - list who created it, how it was shared with other people and what its purpose was.

How interpretations of the past may differ

People who look back on the past often disagree about what they find. They may disagree about all sorts of issues including:

- what actually happened and when
- whether an event or type of behaviour was 'typical' of the period in history when it happened
- why events or developments happened at all or why they happened at a certain time
- which person, factor or consequence was most significant and why
- how much change was happening, how quickly and how it affected different groups of people at the time
- what sources should be used and what they reveal
- what (if anything) we can learn from the events of the past.

Why interpretations of the past may differ

There are many different reasons why people offer different interpretations of the past. Here are a few suggestions:

- They may use different sources, for example someone working at a later date may be able to use newly discovered documents or new scientific techniques to throw more light on the issue.
- They may be faced with gaps in the evidence and may make different but reasonable guesses based on the sources they have.
- They use the same sources very carefully but honestly reach different conclusions.
- They are affected by their own background or context, for example the age in which they were working, their nationality, personality, beliefs and values may all affect their judgements.
- They may be creating their interpretation for different audiences, for example young children or foreign tourists rather than professional historians.
- They may be creating their interpretations for different reasons, for example to provide light-hearted entertainment rather than precise historical understanding.
- They may simply be less careful in applying good historical methods, for example failing to consider all available sources, misunderstanding what sources say, reaching conclusions that cannot be supported by the sources or failing to make their conclusions clear.

Look at the list you made of some historical interpretations that you found in this book (see page 101). Can you see any signs that any were affected by any of the influences listed above?

Exam guidance

This depth study forms the second half of Paper 1: British History. It is worth twenty per cent of your GCSE. The whole exam lasts for 1 hour 45 minutes so you will have just over 50 minutes to answer the four questions on The Norman Conquest.

Question 6a

You will be shown an interpretation of some aspect of the period of the Norman Conquest, 1065–1087. The interpretation may be in text form or an image. The question will start by explaining the point that the interpretation is making. You will have to show that you understand how it does this. The question will usually begin 'In Interpretation A the historian ... Identify and explain one way in which the historian does this.'

Example

6 (a) In Interpretation A the historian Robert Bartlett argues that the 'Harrying of the North' had a powerful impact on northern England. Identify and explain one way in which he does this. (3 marks)

Interpretation A – An extract from the script of *The Normans*, a BBC television series, 2010.

In 1069, William marched on York and crushed the rebellion. The Normans devastated the North of England. They sacked every village and farmstead as they went. Then William divided his troops into smaller bands who destroyed any crops and livestock they could find ... A huge area across northern and central England was laid waste by this 'scorched earth' on the northern rebels. Plotting the settlements destroyed by the Normans shows the scar that was carved across the country by William's army. Sixteen years later, these areas were still desolate wasteland.

Devise five questions like this using five different interpretations that you can find in this book. Try to use images with one or two and text with the others.

Question 6b

For this question you will be asked to suggest an area of further research into an aspect of the historical situation or issue that is the focus of question 6a. You will have to justify the suggestion you make. The question stem will usually be 'If you were asked to do further research on [Interpretation A], what would you choose to investigate? Explain how this would help us to analyse and understand [the topic in 6a].'

Example

6 (b) If you were asked to do further research on one aspect of Interpretation A, what would you choose to investigate? Explain how this would help us to analyse and understand the Harrying of the North. (5 marks)

For each of the questions you invented for 6a, write a brief 6b-style question.

Question 7

Question 7 requires you to explain how far and why two given interpretations differ. A typical stem is 'Interpretations B and C both focus on ... How far do they differ and what might explain any differences?'

Example

7 Interpretations B and C are both illustrations of Norman motte and bailey castles. How far do they differ and what might explain any differences? (12 marks)

Interpretation B – An illustration of the Norman castle at Pickering in Yorkshire by the reconstruction artist Simon Hayfield. The illustration is in the book *Picturing the Past*. The book was published in 1997 and was aimed at adults.

Interpretation C – An illustration of a typical Norman castle in *Living in the Past: The Middle Ages* a history textbook written for primary school children in 1983.

Picture 1 A bailey castle and motte (*mound*)

Preparing for the examination

Question 8/9

You have a choice of two judgement questions. Question 8 or Question 9. These questions in the second part of Paper 1 are the most challenging. They ask you to make a judgement about a particular interpretation of an aspect of the Norman Conquest, 1065–1087. You need to save enough time for this question because it is worth 20 marks.

Example

8 In an article for the *BBC History Magazine* in 2012, the historian Ryan Lavelle argued that late Anglo–Saxon England was 'by no means a 'golden age''. How far do you agree with this view? (20 marks)

9 According to a children's history website, www.MedievalEurope.MrDonn.org, following his victory at Hastings, William 'soon had conquered all of England'. How far do you agree with this view? (20 marks)

Depending on the interpretation given in the question, you may wish to agree completely, disagree completely or take a position where you can see some reasons for agreeing and some for disagreeing. You can get full marks for any of these types of answer provided that you:
- Show that you have understood exactly what the interpretation is claiming.
- Show that you understand any particularly important words, phrases or dates that the interpretation uses.
- Use very clear explanations and suitable, accurate supporting evidence to persuade the examiner that you are giving a very reasonable answer.
- Keep closely to the point all the way through your answer.

In the examples above, are there any words, phrases or dates in the interpretations that you would need to address in your answer?

Choose one of the example questions above and write a plan of how you would answer it. It is helpful to plan each paragraph in your answer so that it has a very definite main point that is clearly supported with accurate and appropriate evidence chosen from your knowledge of the period. Do this planning before you start to write in the exam.

Copyright information:

Interpretation A: Transcribed from BBC 2 series 'The Normans Conquest', presented by Robert Bartlett, 2010. © BBC Publishing Worldwide.

Interpretation B: Reproduced by kind permission of Simon Hayfield, Hayfield Studio, Shustoke UK, www.hayfieldstudio.co.uk

Interpretation C: An illustration of a Norman castle in *Living in the Past: The Middle Ages* a history textbook written for primary school children in 1983. OCR and the publisher are aware that third party material appeared in this sample question paper but it has not been possible to fully identify and acknowledge the source.

Question 8: Quote from Ryan Lavelle, 'The dark side of the Anglo-Saxons', in BBC History Magazine, Vol 13 No. 13, pg 27, 2012. © BBC Publishing.

Question 9: Quote from Lin and Don Donn, The Middle Ages for Kids, www.medievaleurope.mrdonn.org. Accessed January 2015.

Glossary

abbey a place where monks and nuns live and worship

abbot a man in charge of an abbey

accession taking the throne as a king or queen

altar a special table that is used for religious ceremonies, often made of stone

Anglo-Saxons people who lived in England before the Norman Conquest

archaeologist someone who learns about the past by finding and studying the remains of objects and buildings

archbishop a very important Church leader

architecture the design and construction of buildings

archives historical records and documents

artefact an object made by a person

bailey a large enclosed area which was part of a castle

baron a powerful nobleman

Bayeux Tapestry an embroidery telling the story of the Norman Conquest

burh a fortified town built by the Anglo-Saxon kings

burh-geat a fortified dwelling of a Saxon thegn

cathedral a very important church

cavalry soldiers who fight on horseback

ceorl a free Saxon who worked on the land

chronicle a written account, often made by a monk

coronation ceremony when a king or queen is crowned at the beginning of their reign

court the group of people who gathered around the king, wherever he was

culture way of life

Domesday Book a manuscript which records the results of the Domesday Survey

Domesday Survey the process of collecting the information summarised in the Domesday Book

earl a powerful nobleman

earthwork man-made defences created by digging ditches and raising barriers made from the soil and stone

economic to do with money

embroider to decorate fabrics by stitching them with coloured threads

excavation the process of careful digging, as carried out by archaeologists

execute to put someone to death

factor something that plays a part in causing an event or development

fief an area of land held by someone in return for providing services to the lord who owns the land

fyrd the name given to the army of an Anglo-Saxon king

garrison soldiers who lived in and defended a castle

gatehouse a well-defended room built above the entrance to a fort or castle

geld a type of tax

hall the inner part of a castle, where the lord lived

heir person who inherits a property or title when another dies

infantry soldiers who fight on foot

interpretation a version or viewpoint

keep the safest part of a castle

knight an important soldier who served a baron and the king

lord an important person such as a baron or knight

manor an area of land controlled by a lord

manuscript a hand-written document

mercenaries hired soldiers who fight simply to earn money

mint a place where coins are made

monastery a place where monks live and worship

motte a large mound of earth forming part of a castle

nave the part of the church where the people stand or sit for services

nobleman a powerful lord such as a baron

pagan someone who believes in the existence of a wide range of gods or spirits rather than one single god

palisade a fence made of wooden stakes

parchment animal skin used for writing

parish the area served by a church

peasant a poor person who worked on the land

pillage to raid or steal, often with violence

Pope the leader of the Roman Catholic Church

ramparts a defensive wall with a walkway that allows the defenders to move along it

rebel a person who fights against the ruler

relics the remains of a holy person or object often used to help people pray

ringwork an earthwork that forms a circle with wooden defences built on top of it

saint a person whom the Church decides has lived a life of great holiness

sermon a religious talk or lecture

shire a county

succession the arrangement for who should take over following the end of a monarch's reign

successor a person who takes over from another, e.g. as a king or queen

tenant a person who receives land or property in return for money or work

thegn an Anglo-Saxon landowner with enough land to give him quite a high position in society

thrall a slave

vassal a person who holds some land in return for loyal service to a lord or king

villein a peasant who was not free to move away from his lord's manor

wergild the cash value of someone's life in Anglo-Saxon England

witan the powerful lords and bishops who were the advisers to the Anglo-Saxon kings

Index

Alfred Jewel 18
Anglo-Saxon Chronicle 20, 36
Anglo-Saxon England
    artistic reconstruction 24–5
    culture 18–23
    a golden age? 9, 94, 97
    impact of Norman Conquest on 80–93
    religion 14–18
    society in 1065 10–13
Arbo, Peter Nicolai 37
archaeological digs at castle sites 76
art, Anglo-Saxon 18–19
artistic reconstructions 24–5
    Battle Abbey 56
    burhs 21
    castles 62–3, 64, 66, 68, 71, 73, 81
    churches 22
    Tower of London 79
    Westminster Abbey and Palace 23
Asbjørn, brother of Danish king 52, 57

baileys 30, 62
Battle Abbey, East Sussex 41, 56
Battle of Fulford 36
Battle of Hastings 38–41, 42–3
Battle of Stamford Bridge 37
Bayeux Tapestry 6–7, 19, 40–1
'Beowulf' 20
Bible 14
'The Body of Harold' (painting) 95
Brown, Ford Madox 95
buildings
    Anglo-Saxon 21–3
    see also burhs; castles; church buildings
burh-geats 64, 75
burhs 10, 21, 64, 89

Castle Acre, Norfolk 75
castles
    before 1066 in England 21
    early Norman in England 47, 51, 62–3, 65, 66–7
    French 30, 65
    location and appearance 68–71
    studying purpose of 72–7
    Tower of London 78–9
cathedrals 92
ceorls 12, 13, 88
Chepstow Castle, Monmouthshire 69
Church
    English 14–17
    English resistance and reform 56, 92–3
    in Normandy 31
church buildings 15, 22–3, 31, 93
coins 10
Cornwall 10
coronations
    of Queen Matilda 50
    of William the Conqueror 46, 56
counts, French 28, 29
crosses, stone 15
culture, Anglo-Saxon 18–23

Danes 10, 52–3, 57, 58
Domesday Book 70, 82–5
dukes, French 28, 29
Dunstan, St 16

Eagle (comic) 96
Ealdred, Archbishop of York 46, 50, 51, 52
earls, Anglo-Saxon 11, 13
earthworks, surveying 74
Eastern rebellions 1070–71 57–9
Edgar Atheling
    possible successor to throne 33, 34
    and William the Conqueror 45, 46, 47
    rebel 51, 52
Edith, Queen 32
Edric the Wild 47, 53
Edward the Confessor 8–9, 11, 16, 23, 32
Edwin, Earl 36, 46, 47, 51, 58
Elmley Castle, Worcs 74
Ely, Cambs 57, 58–9
England, pre-Norman kingdom of 10
Exeter 48–9, 73
Exeter Book 20

feudal system, French 28, 29
fiefs 28
FitzOsbern, William 46, 47, 52, 68, 69
Forest laws 90
France in 1065 28–31
Fulford, Battle of 36
Fuller brooch 19
fyrd 11, 12

gatehouses 30, 64, 73
geld 89
Goltho castle, Lincs 71
green man carvings 47
Gytha, mother of Harold II 48, 49, 52

Hardrada, Harald 33, 34, 36, 37
Harold II
    Earl of Wessex 11
    succession to throne 32, 33, 34–5
    defence of England and death 36, 37, 38, 39, 40–1
'Harrying of the North' 54–5, 88
Hastings, Battle of 38–41, 42–3
Hastings Castle, East Sussex 66
Hen Domen Castle, Powys 76
Hereward the Wake 57–9
Hereward the Wake – the last of the English (Kingsley) 60–1
The Hobbit (Tolkien) 97

inquests 83
interpretations 6–7, 100–1
    of castles 72–7
    of Edward Confessor's dying words 32
    of the 'Harrying of the North' 55
    of site of Battle of Hastings 42–3
    of succession issue 35
    of 'the Norman Yoke' 94–7
    see also artistic reconstructions

keeps 30
kings, Anglo-Saxon 11, 13
Kingsley, Charles 61
knights 29, 30, 47, 71

land ownership after the Norman conquest 71, 83, 86–7
landscapes and castles 75
Lanfranc, Archbishop 56
language 91
laws 90
literature, Anglo-Saxon 20
London 45, 46

markets 10, 89
Matilda, Queen 31, 50
Mercia 47
monasteries 13, 56, 57, 92
Morcar, Earl 36, 46, 47, 51, 58, 59
Morris, Marcus 96
motte and bailey castles 30, 47, 67, 68, 69, 70, 76
mottes 30, 62, 64, 65, 66, 74
Murdrum Fine 90

Norman Yoke 94–7
Normandy, in 1065 28–31
Northern rebellions 1068–70 50–5

Odo, Bishop of Bayeux 46, 47, 68
Old Sarum, Wilts 80–1

Index

palisades 62
parish churches 93
peasants 12, 88, 94
Pevensey Castle, East Sussex 66

rebellions against Williams the Conqueror
    1066–68 first 46–9
    1068–70 Northern 50–5
    1070–71 in the east 57–9
reconstructions *see* artistic reconstructions
religion in Anglo-Saxon England 14–17
ringworks 30, 67, 69, 74
Robert of Comines 52
Robert of Jumièges 16, 21
Rollo the Walker 27, 28, 31
Roman Catholic Church
    and the English Church 14, 17, 31, 56
    and William the Conqueror 35, 41, 56, 92
Rufus, Alan, Count of Brittany 87, 88

Scotland 10
shires 10
slaves 12, 13, 88
Snorri (Icelandic poet) 37
Stamford Bridge, Battle of 37
Stigand, Archbishop of Canterbury 17, 32, 50, 56
succession crisis 32–5
Svein II, Danish king 52, 57, 58

taxation 85, 89
Textus Roffensis (Book of Rochester) 90–1
thegns 11, 13, 64, 86, 87
thralls (slaves) 12, 13, 88
Tolkien, J.R.R. 97
Tostig (brother of Harold II) 36, 37
Tower of London 78–9
towns
    after the Norman conquest 89
    burhs 10, 21, 64
trade 10, 89
trial by combat 90

uprisings against William the Conqueror
    1066–68 first 46–9
    1068–70 Northern rebellions 50–5
    1070–71 in the east 57–9

vassals 28
Vikings 10, 28, 29, 31
Vitalis, Oderic 46, 47, 54, 94

Wales 10
wergild 13
Wessex 10
Westminster Abbey 23
William the Conqueror
    background of 27, 28, 31
    claim to English throne 33, 34–5
    invasion of England 35, 38, 39, 40, 41
    takes control of England 44–59, 80, 82
    death of 81
Witan 11, 33, 45
women, Anglo-Saxon 13
Wulfstan, Archbishop of York 17

Acknowledgements

Photo credits

p.6–7 © Détail de la Tapisserie de Bayeux - XIème siècle; **p.8** © Reproduced by kind permission of the Syndics of Cambridge University Library; **p.10** © Andrew Cowie/Alamy Stock Photo; **p.11** © United Kingdom, England, The King and his councillor, miniature from the Sacramentarium of Robert de Jumieges, circa 1050/De Agostini Picture Library/G. Dagli Orti/Bridgeman Images; **p.12** t © Cott Tib B V Part 1 f.6 Peasant community working in the fields, from a Calendar, c.1030 (vellum), Anglo-Saxon, (11th century)/British Library, London, UK/British Library Board. All Rights Reserved/Bridgeman Images; **p.12** b © The Trustees of the British Museum; **p.13** © Bodleian Library, MS Junius 11, p.53; **p.14** © British Library/Robana/REX Shutterstock; **p.15** l © Heritage Image Partnership Ltd/Alamy Stock Photo, r © The Trustees of the British Museum; **p.16** © Bodleian Library, auctf432_f1r; **p.17** © World History Archive/Alamy Stock Photo; **p.18** © The Alfred Jewel (gold, rock crystal and enamel) (side view), Anglo-Saxon (9th century)/Ashmolean Museum, University of Oxford, UK/Bridgeman Images; **p.19** t © Granger Historical Picture Archive/Alamy Stock Photo, b © The Trustees of the British Museum; **p.20** © British Library/Robana/REX/Shutterstock; **p.21** © Sciencebloke/publicdomain/https://commons.wikimedia.org/wiki/File:UK-Burh_wall.JPG; **p.22** t © Florian Monheim/Bildarchiv Monheim GmbH/Alamy Stock Photo, b © Reconstruction drawing of St. Peter's Church during the Anglo-Saxon period, Wales, Liam (20th Century) (w/c on paper)/Historic England/Bridgeman Images; **p.23** © Dean and Chapter of Westminster; **p.25** t © Canterbury Archaeological Trust Ltd, b © Historic England Archive; **p.26** © Carolyn Clarke/Alamy Stock Photo; **p.28** © DEA/G. DAGLI ORTI/De Agostini/Getty images; **p.29** Franco Cosimo Panini Editore © Management Fratelli Alinari; **p.30** t and b © Musée de Normandie, Ville de Caen, http://www.musee-de-normandie.caen.fr; **p.31** © DEA/G. DAGLI ORTI/De Agostini/Getty images; **p.32, 34, 35, 36, 38, 40, 41, 65, 66** b © Détail de la Tapisserie de Bayeux - XIème siècle; **p.37** © Battle of Stamford Bridge, 1870 (oil on canvas), Arbo, Peter Nicolai (1831-92)/Private Collection/Photo O. Vaering/Bridgeman Images; **p.39** © Historic England Archive; **p.42–3** © Maurice Savage/Alamy Stock Photo; **p.44** © Look and Learn History Picture Library; **p.46** © Moreleaze Tropicana/Alamy Stock Photo; **p.47** © David Hunter/Alamy Stock Photo; **p.48** © Simon Stapley/Alamy Stock Photo; **p.50** © Serge Angeric/Alamy Stock Photo; **p.51** © travellinglight/Alamy Stock Photo; **p.52** © The death of Aldred, Archbishop of York AD1069, 1920s (litho), Dovaston, Margaret (1884-1954)/Private Collection/Bridgeman Images; **p.54–55** © Rachel Husband/Alamy Stock Photo; **p.56** © Historic England Archive; **p.57** © Science & Society Picture Library/Getty images; **p.58** © Illustration by Jon Cane; **p.59** © Chris Buxton/Alamy Stock Photo; **p.60** © Mary Evans Picture Library; **p.61** © Granger Historical Picture Archive/Alamy Stock Photo; **p.62–3** © In the days of our forefathers, Embleton, Ron (1930-88)/Private Collection/Look and Learn/Bridgeman Images; **p.64** t © Historic England Archive; **p.66** t © Historic England Archive; **p.67** b © Skyscan Balloon Photography.Historic England Archive; **p.68** © Heritage Images/Hulton Archive/Getty images; **p.69** b © Alan Novelli/Alamy Stock Photo; **p.71** © Historic England Archive; **p.73** r illustration from Shiela Sancha, *The Castle Story*, published in 1991 by Kestrel Books; **p.74** © Historic England Archive; **p.75** © Commission Air/Alamy Stock Photo; **p.76** © Clwyd-Powys Archaeological Trust; **p.77** © Détail de la Tapisserie de Bayeux - XIème siècle; **p.78** © Historic Royal Palaces. Photo: James Brittain; **p.79** t © Historic Royal Palaces/High Level Photography Limited; b © Historic Royal Palaces. Drawing Ivan Lapper; **p.80** © robertharding/Last Refuge/Alamy Stock Photo; **p.81** t © Cliff Hide Local/Alamy Stock Photo, b © Historic England/Mary Evans; **p.82** © The National Archives of the UK; **p.84** t © Yuliia Davydenko/123RF, b © The National Archives of the UK; **p.85** © The National Archives of the UK; **p.86** © ICP/incamerastock/Alamy Stock Photo; **p.87** © British Library/Robana/REX Shutterstock; **p.88** © Cott Tib B V f.3 Ploughing, from a Calendar, c.1030 (vellum), Anglo-Saxon, (11th century)/British Library, London, UK/British Library Board. All Rights Reserved/Bridgeman Images; **p.89** © Tony Adebonojo/Alamy Stock Photo; **p.90** t © Textus Roffensis - courtesy of Rochester Cathedral, b © Tony Adebonojo/Alamy Stock Photo; **p.91** © The British Library Board; **p.92** © Angelo Hornak/Alamy Stock Photo; **p.94** © Add 42130 f.170 Man ploughing with oxen, from the 'Luttrell Psalter', c.1325-35 (vellum), English School, (14th century)/British Library, London, UK/British Library Board. All Rights Reserved/Bridgeman Images; **p.95** t © Vivia Decarli/Alamy Stock Photo, b © The Body of Harold Brought Before William the Conqueror, 1844-61 (oil on canvas), Brown, Ford Madox (1821-93)/Manchester Art Gallery, UK/Bridgeman Images; **p.96** © Reproduced with kind permission of the Dan Dare Corporation Limited; **p.97** t © New Line Productions/Photos 12/Alamy Stock Photo, b © Chris Howes/Wild Places Photography / Alamy Stock Photo; **p.104** t © Historic England Archive, b illustration from Greg Thie, *Living in the Past: The Middle Ages*, published in 1983 by Simon & Schuster Education.